THE LAW AND POLITICAL PROTEST

"The power of school authorities to regulate political activities of students and faculty, are of particular concern to our state and nation today. Education is in a state of ferment, if not turmoil . . . it is imperative that the courts carefully differentiate in treatment those who are violent and heedless of the rights of others . . . and those whose concerns are no less burning but who seek to express themselves through peaceful, orderly means. In order to discourage persons from engaging in the former type of activity, the courts must take pains to assure that the channels of peaceful communication remain open and that peaceful activity is fully protected."

Los Angeles Teachers Union vs. Los Angeles Board of Education, 78 California Reporter at 732 (1969)

THE LAW AND POLITICAL PROTEST:

A Handbook on Your Rights Under the Law

Tom Dove, Senior Editor
with thirty second and
third year law students,
Boalt Hall School of Law,
University of California
(Berkeley)

WORLD WITHOUT WAR COUNCIL

SBN 912018-08-9
First Printing, May 1970, 2,500
Second Edition, September 1970, 10,000
Cover design by Jack Stauffacher
Inside art work by Gar Smith
Printed in the United States of America
for the Inter-Council Publications Committee

World Without War Council
1730 Grove Street, Berkeley, California 94709

PREFACE

This book is the product of the skill and commitment of a number of students at Boalt Hall (The University of California's Law School at Berkeley) who sought to provide the public with a detailed guide to the legal limits of political protest and political action in the United States. The World Without War Council has performed a useful public service in publishing it.

The aim of the book is to describe the law as accurately and objectively as possible. Quite properly, therefore, it does not attempt to take partisan stands on the varieties of political conduct which it discusses. Nor does it purport to reflect on the significance of the total framework of freedoms and restraints which it describes. But it provides the concerned reader with both the occasion and the material for such reflection.

For myself, perhaps because I am over thirty—well, well, over thirty—the law seems to make generous provision for dissent and political action. It strikes me that, taken as a whole, our law has gone a good distance toward fulfilling the democratic commitment of protecting freedom for dissenting political speech and conduct and, of equal importance, of providing recourse for those who believe their freedoms have been abridged.

But whether my overall assessment is right or not is not of great moment. Many will argue that in this or that respect, or in many respects, the law is too restrictive, that it is too resistant to new and desirable forms of political action, that some of our laws give too much authority to government and its officials. I have no difficulty with this criticism. Indeed, I have my own prescription for reform. Nor do I have difficulty with the view that the law-in-action gives less freedom than the law-in-books and that the organization of society and the distribution of authority, formal and informal, mar the fulfillment of the promise of freedom. Our society and its legal structures stand only to profit from criticism of this kind.

What is indeed disturbing is not conduct and criticism aimed at enlarging the ambit for dissent and controversy, but that which rejects the value of the open society in favor of particular substantive goals as perceived by a particular few. I speak of those—sometimes among the otherwise more sensitive and gifted of our young—who are so moved by their perception of wrong and injustice and so utterly convinced of the righteousness of their cause and of the rightness of their way that they are prepared to stifle those who disagree, to assault, to bombard with rocks, even to burn and bomb. They cannot realize their vision of the good in these ways. They can only generate a chaos and dehumanization from which no Phoenix will arise, only arrogant repression by those who end up with the physical power to enforce their own vision of the true, whether those turn out to be the insurrectionists themselves or, which is far more likely, those who rise up against them. This has always been the way with holy wars. One need recall only the Crusades and the Inquisition.

So long as men are men they will have different visions of what is their due and others', and what is right and true. The condition of civilization is acceptance of a means of living with each other's passions and follies. In personal terms this means some humility, some sense that we may be mistaken, as so many have been before us, and a decent respect for the opinions and claims of others. In political terms this means a commitment to the processes of democratic change and the open society as overriding any particular substantive goal. Without these commitments it must be as Matthew Arnold said, when the world,

Hath really neither joy, nor love, nor light,
Nor certitude, nor peace, nor help for pain;
And we are here as on a darkling plain
Swept with confused alarms of struggle and flight,
Where ignorant armies clash by night.

Sanford H. Kadish*

---

*Professor of Law, University of California, Berkeley and National President, American Association of University Professors.

TABLE OF CONTENTS

INTRODUCTION

ALMOST EVERYONE is aware that the United States Constitution guarantees to him some basic rights of free speech, of assembly and of petition for redress of grievances. However, a civics class knowledge that you have a right to "free speech" does not tell you whether this protects you when you hand out leaflets in a shopping center parking lot or whether you may be suspended for wearing a black protest armband to school. This handbook attempts to explain what these constitutional freedoms mean in practical rules which apply to your political activities. These constitutional doctrines are complex, often vague and may give even the experienced political activist grave cause for concern as he attempts to sort them out, especially if they remain couched in legalistic jargon. This handbook approaches these doctrines from a grassroots level and sets out rules for circulating petitions, participating in rallies, handing out leaflets, etc. It states in a concise manner what your legal rights are, and what legal limitations can and have been imposed upon their exercise.

The emphasis of certain sections of the book, in particular the sections on students, faculty and staff, is on the laws of the State of California because of our familiarity with these laws and because, more often than not, they exemplify national practices. It is, however, good advice to look up your own campus rules and regulations and make any necessary changes. The other areas of the handbook are more or less applicable nationwide, for it is a principle of the law that questions concerning what constitutes a violation of one's constitutional rights are federal questions, that is, in the last outcome a federal standard shall be applied. While this means that a federal court's decision can and does supersede any state court interpretation, the case can take a long time to reach the federal courts on any of these issues. This prompts us to advise you now, as we do in the section on *If You Are Arrested,* of the cardinal rule of protest: unless you want to get arrested—Don't.

This book emphasizes your legal rights under the First Amendment as interpreted in current laws. It does not consider the arguments which have been made for bringing a test case or for other activity of questionable legality. Some forms of civil disobedience can aid in the protection and extension of democratic freedoms.* Acts which deny the authority of the law, which teach contempt for it, which refuse to accept the consequences of illegal acts are frequently misnamed civil disobedience today. Acts of insurrectionary violence or proto-revolutionary activity can readily create condi-

---

*A basic introduction to the literature on civil disobedience is the World Without War Council's bibliography, "Civil Disobedience and the American Democratic Tradition." Among the available reprints on the subject are Harris Wofford's "A Lawyer's Case for Civil Disobedience," Gene Sharp's "Civil Disobedience in a Democracy," Carl Cohen's "The Essence and Ethics of Civil Disobedience," Robert Pickus' "Civil Disobedience and Insurrectionary Violence," Harry Prosch's "Limits to the Moral Claim in Civil Disobedience," and Richard Wasserstrom's "The Obligation to Obey the Law." All of these reprints may be obtained from the World Without War Council.

tions in which the law is not an effective instrument in resolving conflicts. The law clearly distinguishes between civil disobedience and insurrectionary violence. If your preference is for protecting against governmental repression the broad range of political protest channels which are open and if your preference is for resolving disputes through legal means, rather than through violence, then it is important to acts in ways consonant with those beliefs.

This handbook is the result of research undertaken during and since the outburst of student political protest which followed the U.S. invasion of Cambodia. As students and other concerned individuals spread out into the general community in an attempt to help end the war in Southeast Asia, the Boalt Hall School of Law at the Berkeley campus of the University of California was deluged with a wave of inquiries regarding the state of the law affecting a citizen's right to engage in any of the myriad forms of political protest. In response to these requests, the Research Staff of the Boalt Hall Action Committee set out to compile this desired, yet heretofore not readily available information. It is our hope that this handbook can provide a clear, understandable and useful outline of the law for concerned citizens from all walks of life who are interested in exercising their right to dissent.

The entire staff involved in the production of this handbook has been well aware of the importance of providing accurate and understandable information about the state of the law. We have had a recurring nightmare of thousands of people getting busted for taking our advice. While a sincere effort has been made to be correct at every point, we are only human and it is possible that errors have gone by our scrutiny. It should also be pointed out now, as it will be throughout the text, that the law does change. The judiciary has shown their competence and ability to lead as well as follow society's markings. For this reason among others, if you are engaged in organizing political action, it is wise to seek out legal advice from the planning through and after the execution stages.

*　　*　　*　　*　　*　　*

The material in this book was prepared by the Boalt Hall Action Committee, formed in May 1970 to further anti-war and community action activities. The research staff for this book was made up of thirty members of the second and third year classes at Boalt Hall School of Law. Professors Phillip Johnson and Michael E. Smith of the Boalt Hall Law School faculty read and criticized the manuscript at various stages of preparation. Tom Dove, a third year law student, served as senior editor. The Boalt Hall Action Committee is solely responsible for the final contents. In addition to this book, the Committee has also published a *Handbook on the War in Southeast Asia* which is available for $.50 from the Boalt Hall Action Committee, Box 4000 E, Sather Gate Station, Berkeley, California 94704.

August, 1970　　　　　　**Tom Dove**
Berkeley, California　　Boalt Hall Action Committee

CHAPTER ONE

YOUR RIGHTS

The primary source of legal protection of most of your rights to engage in political protest is found in the language of the First Amendment to the Constitution which provides that "Congress shall make no law . . . abridging the freedom of speech, or of the press; or the right of the people to peaceably assemble, and to petition the government for a redress of grievances." The constitutions of each and every state contain similar guarantees (California Constitution Article 1, § 1; New York Constitution Article 1, § 8, etc.), but the real power behind these guarantees lies in the fact that the Due Process Clause of the 14th Amendment to the Federal Constitution incorporates this protection of speech, press, petition and assembly from state action which would violate these rights.

While the terse language of the First Amendment has been interpreted by the Supreme Court over the years in a manner which gives you a right to engage in a wide variety of political protest activities, these rights are not unlimited; they can be and have been subjected to a variety of limitations. It is not necessary to go into any long-winded rhetoric to explain that "freedom of speech" does not include the right to falsely yell "fire" in the proverbial crowded theater. Moreover, the fact that you have a constitutionally protected right to engage in an activity does not mean that that right will necessarily be respected by law enforcement officials. There are at present literally hundreds of state and local laws which are unconstitutional on their face because they are unclear, vague and too broad, and as a result punish what should be protected activity. Also you are certain to encounter frequently local officials and private citizens who, out of fear, ignorance or hostility, will attempt to curtail even clearly legitimate activities. Thus you, as have your many predecessors in previous confrontations, will often have to choose between foregoing or at least postponing your activities, or testing the legality of the statute or the actions of the enforcement officials in a court case. This is a warning, one that should be ever present in your mind as you read over the following delineation of your rights and as you attempt to put them in practice.

I. Political Demonstrations and Rallies

Tactical Advice: If you are planning any massive organized protest, be it a march, a rally, a sit-in or whatever, and the urgency of your cause is not so great as to prevent including a legal counsel in your planning, then by all means get a lawyer or law student in on the ground floor. The problems are many, and a hired legal consultant might be worthwhile in aiding you and your fellows in avoiding legal pitfalls along the way. If your action is immediate or spontaneous or if you are merely one of the ever growing numbers of initiates in this area of political activity, then the following account of your rights may help you.

The First Amendment guarantees you the right to assemble peacefully with fellow citizens and to engage

in political demonstrations in *appropriate public* areas such as streets and parks. The key words above are *appropriate* and *public.* The First Amendment also protects you from official reprisals for expressing unpopular political views at such gatherings. In explaining the First Amendment's scope, the Supreme Court has stated that your speech is protected and you cannot be prevented from engaging in these activities *unless* "the words used are used in such circumstances and are of such a nature as to create a *clear and present danger* that they will bring about substantive evils that Congress (or a state legislature) has the right to prevent," *Schenck v. U.S.,* 249 U.S. 47, (1919), per Justice Holmes concurring. While it is often very difficult to determine just what language can constitute such a punishable "clear and present danger," it is clear that actual physical violence or the immediate and imminent threat of violence can present such a punishable danger. In its very latest pronouncement on the question, the Supreme Court stated in *Brandenburg v. Ohio,* 395 U.S. 444, (1969) that "the constitutional guarantees of free speech and free press do not permit a state to forbid or proscribe *advocacy* of the use of force or of law violation *except* where such advocacy is directed to inciting or producing imminent lawless action and is *likely* to incite or produce such action." Thus if you are at a demonstration it is often the context of the words in a speech and the mood of the audience which are relevant factors in determining whether or not your words, regardless of how harsh or insensitive they might be in themselves, are creating a serious danger for which you may be constitutionally punished. This is generally regarded as a "balancing test" that the court will later apply to your language in light of all of the circumstances. The mere fact that in the lawful exercise of your right to speak, you presented views that "set off" a hostile audience who then threatened violence is *not* sufficient to remove the protection of the law from your speech. When we are only concerned with the language issue, you are generally safe unless you view the words as an incitement to riot, or if they would be "fighting words" if someone spoke them to you, i.e., if the general audience reacted to the speech by rioting. If the speech only incites "fringe elements" to riot, or if the audience has an unduly hostile tone not of your own creation, then it is the duty of law enforcement officials to restrain the disruptive elements in your audience and to protect your right to speak. As Mr. Justice Douglas stated in *Terminello v. Chicago,* 337 U.S. 1, 4, (1949),

Accordingly a function of free speech under our system of government is to invite dispute. It may indeed best serve its high purpose when it induces a condition of unrest, creates dissatisfaction with conditions as they are, or even stirs people to anger. Speech is often provocative and challenging. It may strike at prejudices and preconceptions and have profound unsettling effects as it presses for the acceptance of an idea. That is why freedom of speech, though not absolute, is nevertheless protected against censorship or punishment, unless shown likely to produce a clear and present danger of a serious substantive evil that rises far above public inconvenience, annoyance or unrest.

Thus while it is clear that demonstrations or rallies cannot be completely prohibited unless they really create a "clear and present danger," they certainly can be and are subjected to reasonable restrictions, not related solely to the context of the speech, designed to protect the rights of others and those of the community at large. There are many policy factors used to justify the "reasonable" regulation of free speech activities in public areas such as: keeping the streets and sidewalks open and safe for general traffic, preserving peace and order, and in limiting to some extent the amount of noise and inconvenience caused by these activities. In short, a city may require a permit to hold a parade, rally, etc., and can impose "reasonable" restrictions on the time, place, and manner involved in holding the demonstration. However, the Supreme Court has not and does not allow such permits to be used as a tool of censorship or prohibition of unpopular ideas; no state can grant any state or local official *discretionary* power to grant or deny such permits in a manner that would constitute censorship of the content of the speech to be presented. Generally, if a municipality or school board, or other public regulatory agency *customarily* allows the free use of its buildings or facilities for public meetings, then such body cannot deny that use to any group advocating an unpopular idea unless that body can clearly demonstrate that the particular meeting would pose a "clear and present danger" of violence and/or property destruction, *Schneider v. Irvington,* 308 U.S. 147 (1939); *In re Hoffman,* 67 Cal. 2d 853 (1967) citing *Danskin v. San Diego Unified School District,* 28 Cal. 2d 536, 171 P. 2d 885 (1946).

If you are organizing a demonstration or rally be sure to check your local city and/or school regulations for time, place and manner restrictions and permit requirements; as for municipal regulations, this information is usually attainable by calling the city clerk. Should you be denied a permit, contact your nearest legal assistance office or the American Civil Liberties Union if you do not have your own lawyer to initiate immediate legal action. It is very likely that you will be able to get a court injunction very quickly to restrain the authorities from interfering with your activities if the location for which you seek the permit has in the past been the site for other, less controversial rallies.

II. Leafletting, Handbilling and Use of Sound Equipment

Leafletting and handbilling—the poor man's press—are time-honored methods of expressing and communicating political dissent, and best of all, they are protected by the First Amendment. Thus you have a constitutional right to pass out *non-commercial* leaflets in purely public areas such as streets, sidewalks and public parks and, under recent decisions of the United States Supreme Court, in "quasi-public" areas such as shopping center parking lots, *Amalgamated Food Employees Union v. Logan Valley Plaza,* 391 U.S. 308 (1968). What is a "quasi-public" area for free speech protection purposes is sometimes a debatable question, but the trend of decisions indicates that parking lots, entrances to shopping centers and supermarkets, the insides of railway stations, bus terminals and subway stations as well as open air mall areas of *un*-enclosed shopping center complexes are all areas that, while privately owned, have acquired a "public" character due to the nature of modern business and transportation. As a result speech must be protected and allowed in these areas; otherwise a large percentage of any audience which you might be seeking to contact would be placed beyond your reach. A more difficult question is presented when the issue is whether you can leaflet inside a totally enclosed shopping mall, a modern form of "city center" shopping. There are conflicting views in different states; New York and Oregon cases seem to say you have such a right while a recent Court of Appeals case in Southern California says that this type of complex is *not* "quasi-public," and therefore you can be excluded. The advice of the editor here is to check the law in your own state on this point and remember that at all times it is a wise tactic to seek the management's permission in advance of beginning your activities.

[11]

LEAFLETTING AND HANDBILLING

Often supermarket or shopping centers will refuse permission to leaflet on their "private" property. First call the manager of the store or center involved and explain that you would like permission to hand out leaflets near the door but that you will *in no way* interfere with the ingress of customers into the store, other than to offer them leaflets, or petitions on clipboards, or engage them in conversation. He may ask whether you will be responsible for clearing up the leaflets. Don't get trapped. Say that you cannot be responsible if *his* customers drop papers on *his* property. Tell him that you believe you have a constitutional right to pass out leaflets, even though it is "technically" private property and even though it may create some small inconvenience. Probably he will be unimpressed by this legal argument, but it is worth a try. *Be sure to get his name;* it will help when talking to his superiors.

If the store is not part of a chain, try to get the name of the store's attorney. If the manager won't give it to you, then tell him you are prepared to sue him and his store for an injunction and for damages for violation of your civil rights, and that you believe it would be much easier and would save him a lot of time and money if you could just discuss it with the store's attorney. If he still won't give you the attorney's name, try to talk to someone else above (or below) him who will. You might be able to get a secretary to tell you if you don't tell her what it is about.

If the store is part of a chain, get the name of someone higher up and if you meet resistance at that level (as you probably will) then try to get the name of the chain's attorney or legal counsel.

When you reach the attorney, explain that you think there are legal rights involved and that you would appreciate it if he would look over the precedents establishing the right. Explain the holdings of the key cases to him. Try to sound reasonable and responsible. Assure him that there will be no disruption. You might even say that if any leafletters act disruptively at his store you will be willing to talk to them to explain that they have no legal right to do so. It probably won't be necessary to explain that you are considering sueing, but you may have to. In all probability, he will agree with you once he has had a chance to look over the cases. If so, then ask him if he will call the manager involved to tell him of your rights.

If cornered and you feel you want to leaflet an enclosed mall shopping center despite the denial of your request for permission, an "educated guess" would be that the Federal Courts in your District would vindicate your rights, but remember that could be a long and tedious test case.

You may *not* engage in leafletting or handbilling on private property which does not have the "quasi-public" character mentioned above, i.e., you cannot hand out leaflets *inside* a department or grocery store. Neither may you conduct these activities upon a person's private property, *vacant or occupied,* if "NO TRESPASSING" notices are posted or if the owner has in any other manner indicated that your presence is not welcome. (See also subsection IV for the door-to-door solicitation rule.)

While your right to leaflet on public property and "quasi-public" property is broad, it is certainly not absolute. You may never obstruct the passage of pedestrians or customers when you are leafletting or you may lose the right to do so. Also, *never, never* force a leaflet upon a person because, if he or she should really care to press a point and the police are unsympathetic to your cause, you might well find yourself arrested on a charge of assault and battery. Tactic: stand by the entrance and hand out leaflets to customers as they enter or leave, don't chase them, don't force the issue and above all, don't prevent them from entering or leaving by blocking the entrance or exit in any fashion.

There is a restriction on leafletting in a purely "public place" if that public place happens to be one *not* normally held open to the general public, e.g., a jailhouse or a military installation, or any other restricted government installation. When dealing with these locations the Court has consistently held that there is *no* public right to enter upon these grounds for the purpose of exercising your First Amendment rights, that is, you can be totally excluded from these grounds, *Adderly v. Florida,* 385 U.S. 39, (1970).

Municipalities may impose reasonable time, place and manner restrictions on your handbilling activities just as they may regulate parades, etc., but once again their right to restrict your actions is limited. A local ordinance may limit your actions to certain times and require a permit, but just as with rallies, the permit cannot be denied because of the content of the leaflet. The power to grant or deny these permits must be conditioned on standards reasonably related to traffic control, public safety, etc., and these standards must be *applied* non-discriminatorily. Just as with the parade question, if others have regularly received permission under the ordinance, and your request to leaflet is denied, an injunction will most likely lie against the discriminating officials, *Cox v. Louisiana,* 377 U.S. 288 (1965). The officials may not require you to print the name of your group, the distributor, on the leaflet unless the material contains an attack on a public officer or candidate, *Talley v. California,* 362 U.S. 60 (1960), because to do so would tend to restrict your freedom of expression, i.e., it would have a "chilling effect" on speech which the Constitution will not normally permit.

Usually, the fact that the recipients of your leaflets discard them and create a litter problem is not sufficient cause to deny you your right to distribute leaflets. Local authorities may certainly invoke anti-litter ordinances against persons who actually drop the leaflets, but not against those who distribute them, *Schneider v. Irvington,* 308 U.S. 147 (1939). However, the authorities may prevent you from distributing the leaflets in a manner which will in itself create a litter problem, and many cities have ordinances prohibiting the random posting of leaflets, or placing them on unattended vehicles.

While the leaflet and handbill are "time-honored" methods, the use of sound amplification equipment to put across a protest message at rallies, parades and the like has become more and more commonplace, and consequently has become a source for many of the "Breach of the Peace" convictions that plague demonstrators. Sound trucks, bullhorns and similar equipment can be illegal as a "public nuisance" if they are used to emit *any* message amplified to a "loud and raucous volume," even if the message is patently of public concern and interest. The idea here is that even though there is a public policy favoring free speech, such interest can be outweighed by the general community interest in order and tranquility. Thus, while there can be no absolute ban on the use of such equipment in purely public places (watch out for school and university regulations in this area), the law does allow time, place and manner ordinances which restrict the use of these electronic aids when they could be termed a public nuisance, *Kovacs v. Cooper,* 336 U.S. 77 (1949).

III. Card Tables

When collecting petition signatures or passing out literature, it is often helpful to set up a card table. Unfortunately, you do not have a constitutionally pro-

tected right in California to set up card tables on sidewalks or in other public areas, *People v. Amdur,* 123 Cal. App. 2d 951, 194 P. 2d 588 (1954). Thus, municipalities may completely prohibit the use of card tables. While some recent cases in other jurisdictions indicate that this rule may be wrong, it has not yet been overruled in California, *Wolin v. Port of N.Y. Authority,* 392 F 2d 83 (1968); *People v. Katz,* 21 N.Y. 2d 132 (1967). The situation is not altogether bleak, however. Some municipalities do have ordinances authorizing the use of card tables which block no more than a specified portion of the sidewalk. If a city by ordinance or by custom does permit card tables, it may not arbitrarily or discriminatorily deny such permission to particular individuals or groups. In addition, many shopping center managers will allow card tables upon request. If allowed, card tables may presumably be used for any activities protected by the First Amendment and carried out without creating an obstruction, hazard, or great inconvenience because of the location of the tables.

IV. Door-To-Door Canvassing

You have a legal right to engage in door-to-door canvassing for the purpose of discussing political issues and for distributing non-commercial literature. However, a state or municipality can regulate such activity in a non-discriminatory fashion and the law may require you to notify the police or to obtain a permit before you canvass—*particularly if you are collecting money.* If your canvassing efforts include the sale of any materials, such as informational treatises, then you will normally be required to obtain some form of peddler's license. In either case, a municipality cannot impose a license tax on your efforts (if you are *not* involved in

any selling efforts) nor can any official have the complete discretionary power to deny permits when and where necessary. Again, non-discriminatory, reasonable guidelines must be established and followed in granting or denying such permits. It will be important for you to check the local ordinances of each community that you will canvass for its applicable regulations, especially since municipalities can and do regulate door-to-door solicitations and canvassing by making it a crime to ring the doorbell or in any other way bother someone who has clearly indicated that he does not want to be disturbed by posting a sign to that effect. The chief cases in this area are *Cantwell v. Connecticut,* 310 U.S. 296 (1940); *Largent v. Texas,* 318 U.S. 418 (1943); and *Martin v. City of Struthers,* 319 U.S. 141 (1943), which all combined hold that a city cannot absolutely prohibit door-to-door canvassing.

V. Petitions

Your First Amendment right to petition the government for redress of grievances includes both the right to collect signatures and to sign petitions yourself. The rules governing leafletting and door-to-door canvassing (see sections III & IV above) also apply to the circulation of petitions. Thus, there is a constitutionally protected right to collect signatures on a street or by going from door-to-door.

There are two general types of petitions:

A. *Informal*

You have a right to sign or to send an informal petition to any official or to any branch of the government (or to anyone else for that matter). Petitions can be on most any subject, but you are responsible for any charges and allegations of illegal activity contained in any petition that you sign. Therefore be certain of charges made or pay the consequences. While an informal petition to a court does not appear on its face to be in any explicit manner an improper activity, there is at least one state court decision in Wisconsin, *In re Stolen,* 216 N.W. 127 (1927), which has held that the use of a petition in an attempt to influence a court on a pending case is an abuse of the right of petition and is an activity not within the protection of the First Amendment.

There are no formal requirements for an informal petition, anyone can sign. However, it is a good practice to have each page contain the statement of purpose or intent at the top followed by neatly ordered columns of numbered lines for signatures. The petition may include other such items as the date or the signer's address, but these are purely optional. Completed informal petitions need no certification or approval.

B. *Formal*

In addition to the informal petition discussed above, most states have made allowance for a formal petition procedure which in most cases tends to be a highly technical and elaborate process, thus making it very difficult to accomplish correctly without legal advice. Under these formal systems of voter petitions one can, by collecting the requisite number of signatures in the prescribed manner: (1) initiate legislation and have it placed on the ballot at a general election (Initiative); (2) submit legislation enacted by the legislature to the voters for approval or rejection at a general election (Referendum); and (3) remove elected public officers (Recall). These procedures are available at the county and city levels as well as the state level, and all require the filing of formal petitions which must meet a

number of requirements as to form and content. For example, the California Constitution and the Election Code contain comprehensive provisions (see references below) dealing with the form, preparation, circulation, and filing of these petitions. These provisions should be consulted by anyone interested in utilizing these measures.

It is more likely that you will be involved in circulating or signing such petitions than in preparing them. There are a number of formal requirements that you should be familiar with if you are signing or soliciting signatures for voter petitions. The California requirements, typical of many such systems, outlined below apply to petitions involving statewide measures; the requirements for county and city petitions are substantially similar.

1. Formal Requirements. The petitions may be done in sections; however, each section must contain a correct copy of the title and text at the top [CAL ELECTIONS CODE § 3510]. The signer must be a registered, qualified voter of the county in which the petition is being circulated and he must supply, in adddition to his signature, his address and the date upon which he signs [CAL ELECTIONS CODE § 45]. His precinct number must also appear, but it does not have to be supplied by the voter himself.

Every individual who solicits petition signatures must submit an affidavit attesting to his qualifications as a voter in the county in which he solicited and verifying that, to the best of his knowledge, the signatures are genuine [CAL ELECTIONS CODE § 3513]. He must also supply his voting address [CAL ELECTIONS CODE § 47].

2. Penalties. There are severe criminal penalties for abuse of the petition process. You can be fined up to $5,000 and sentenced to jail for up to two years for: filing or circulating petitions which contain signatures

you know to be false; signing a petition more than once; signing it if you are not qualified; or misrepresenting the contents or effects of the petition to induce someone to sign [CAL ELECTIONS CODE §§ 29210-29226].

The following constitutional and statutory provisions govern the procedures for Initiative, Referendum, and Recall in California:

Initiative:
    State: CAL CONSTITUTION, Article 4, § 22
               CAL ELECTIONS CODE §§ 3500-3523
    County: CAL ELECTIONS CODE §§ 3700-3721
    City: CAL ELECTIONS CODE §§ 4000-4023

Referendum:
    State: CAL CONSTITUTION, Article 4, § 23
               CAL ELECTIONS CODE §§ 3500-3523
    County: CAL ELECTIONS CODE §§ 3750-3754
               CAL ELECTIONS CODE §§ 4050-4057

Recall:
    State: CAL CONSTITUTION, Article 4, § 23
               CAL ELECTIONS CODE §§ 2700-2704
    County: CAL ELECTIONS CODE §§ 27200-27216
    City: CAL ELECTIONS CODE §§ 27500-27521

VI. Picketing

Peaceful picketing is another form of protest activity protected by the guarantees of freedom of speech and assembly; thus you have a constitutional right to appear in groups in proper areas with placards which express your views and appeal for public support. However, picketing does involve something more than "pure speech" and as such the courts will allow addi-

tional restrictions upon this activity which they will not allow upon pure speech, to prevent the picketing from becoming disruptive, *Brotherhood v. Hanke,* 399 U.S. 470, (1950).

Picketing will lose its constitutional protection if it becomes violent, if it is enmeshed with contemporaneous violent conduct, if it unduly hampers the flow of traffic in or out of the target building, or if it significantly obstructs normal operations in that building or surrounding buildings, *Milk Wagon Drivers Union v. Meadowmoor Dairies,* 312 U.S. 287 (1941). State or local statutes can also make it unlawful for pickets to obstruct pedestrian or vehicular traffic on the public streets. If you are engaged in one of these unlawful forms of picketing activity, you may be arrested for trespass or for disorderly conduct (such as failure to disperse when so ordered).

The law remains dishearteningly unclear as to exactly where picketing is or is not permissible. Your right to engage in peaceful, unobstructive picketing activity on public streets, in public parks, on a state capitol's surrounding grounds, and in the "public areas" such as parking lots of certain commercial establishments (see above the discussion of "quasi-public property") seems to be clear. The real problem lies with the legal view that not all public facilities may be picketed if the court should decide that such places are inappropriate for picketing and other forms of political demonstration. If such an area is one used almost exclusively for governmental activity and is not *normally* held open to the general public (i.e., a jail house, or the chambers of a state assembly, etc.), then the state or municipality concerned may apparently utilize its trespass laws to prohibit picketing or demonstrations, *Adderly v. Florida,* 385 U.S. 39 (1966). You can also be prevented from picketing a court house if your purpose is to affect the outcome of a pending case.

The law does allow you to picket organizations or commercial establishments so long as the object of your picketing is legal. Thus you may picket a supermarket to protest its hiring practices, but you would not be protected if your purpose were to demand that the management engage in illegal discrimination in hiring. If your picketing has a legal purpose, then proceed, but remember it may never obstruct the entrances to a building or interfere physically with the use of the target building by employees or customers of the establishment. If it does obstruct, the management can and will obtain an injunction (an order from a court) limiting the number and location of the participating pickets, *San Diego Gas and Electric Co. v. CORE,* 241 Cal App. 2d 405, 50 Cal. Rptr. 638 (1966).

VII. Consumer Boycotts

The organization of a consumer boycott is a lawful method of exerting economic pressure, and thus voicing protest of a political sort under the legal systems of California and other states, witness the recent successful conclusion of the five-year-old grape boycott. In order to remain lawful both the goals of the boycott and the methods by which it is carried out must be legitimate. There are very, very few court decisions concerning the legality of boycotts that are not completely tied up with labor unions and inextricably enmeshed with the complexities of labor law. Thus, if you are setting out to organize a boycott, local, regional or national, get a lawyer to help you through your planning stages. Of course, there are no legal limitations upon your ability to respect a boycott by not buying from the target company.

THE LAW AND POLITICAL PROTEST

A. *Legality: The Means*

Boycotts may legally be promoted via picketing, leafletting, newspaper and other forms of advertising, etc. in accordance with the rules covering those particular activities. There are no special rules affecting these activities when they are carried on to further a boycott. Thus, you can picket to effectuate a boycott, but the picketing cannot be disruptive, violent or destructive. The media, such as newspaper ads, can be used to announce your actions so long as the message contains no false or misleading statements which might subject you to libel laws.

B. *Legality: The Ends of a Boycott*

There is little law on just what constitutes a legitimate end for a boycott, so this can be a tricky question to be answered at the planning stage. Apparently you can boycott a commercial establishment to attempt to persuade it to change its buying policies ("Don't Buy California Table Grapes"), but you cannot use a boycott to injure or damage a business as *punishment* for a past act (i.e., because the store had, up until now, carried a boycotted article), *N.A.A.C.P. v. Overstreet,* 221 Ga. 16, 142 S.E. 2d 816 (1965). Nor can you use a boycott in an attempt to force a store or organization to do something which is against statutory law or against public policy as that policy has been *judicially* stated. For example, the United States Supreme Court has held that you can be stopped from picketing a supermarket if the "end" of such action is to force the management to hire a set percentage of minority workers, *Hughes v. Superior Court,* 339 U.S. 460 (1950). On the other hand, boycott activities are generally permissible if the goal *conforms* with the policy of the law (e.g., prohibition of racial discrimination) and merely seeks to accelerate commercial or organizational compliance.

VIII. Draft Card Protests

The burning or turning in of draft cards has become a fairly popular form of protest in recent years. Either act constitutes the same offense—nonpossession—and results in the same consequences at law. Thus there is no additional penalty for burning, but the government may be more likely to prosecute someone who burns a card in public than a person who simply turns his in. While the possible penalties are severe, the practical consequences depend on the Justice Department's current policies.

If you are a registrant between 18 and 35, failure to have your draft card and classification card in your possession is punishable by a $10,000 fine and 5 years in prison or both (32 Code of Federal Regulations § § 1617.1, 1623.5). The United States Supreme Court has held this law constitutional, *United States v. O'Brien,* 391 U.S. 367 (1968).

In the past, draft card protesters were seldom prosecuted. Instead, the Justice Department turned over the names of violators to Selective Service officials who then reclassified and drafted the violators. The Supreme Court recently declared this scheme illegal, *Gutnecht v. United States,* 396 U.S. 295 (1970), and now the government's only recourse is prosecution.

Sources inside the U.S. Attorney's office say that the Justice Department in Washington has issued a directive requiring clearance from them before any prosecution is initiated. There is reason to believe that there will be no prosecutions for this offense alone, as the number of such cases is staggering and would result in overburdening both the U.S. Attorney's office and the federal courts. Most likely, U.S. Attorneys will wait until a protestor refuses induction and then indict him on two counts—nonpossession and refusing induction. In any case, the ultimate decision will come from Washington and at this date is still forthcoming.

IX. Tax Refusal

A recently much discussed method of political protest is refusing to pay taxes. It is, of course, illegal and the potential penalties for such action are severe. However, the practical consequences are less onerous due to the difficulty and expense involved in the government's bringing a suit.

A. *Federal Income Tax*

Willfully submitting false information to an employer regarding the amount of income to be withheld from salary is punishable by a fine of $500, one year in prison, or both (Internal Revenue Code, § 7205) and a civil penalty of $50 for each false statement (IRC § 6683). There are no known prosecutions resulting in fine or imprisonment, but the civil penalty is often imposed. Employers are under a duty to report suspected false statements to the Internal Revenue Service.

Willful failure to pay federal income taxes is a misdemeanor, with a maximum penalty of one year in jail, or $10,000 fine, or both plus the cost of prosecution (IRC § 7203). In the last 20 years, only seven income tax refusers have been prosecuted, six of them filed no tax return or a false one. Apparently the IRS strongly prefers the non-criminal sanctions (see C below). However, if tax refusal becomes massive, prosecutions are not inconceivable. If you should decide to refuse payment of your taxes, be sure that you *do* file

a return as the chances of prosecution are greater if you do not.

B. *Federal Telephone Tax*

Your telephone service probably would not be cut off by the telephone company for failure to pay the tax. The phone company has no real interest in collection since it is not required to produce the tax if the consumer fails to pay. It is required, however, to report such failure to the IRS.

As with income tax, failure to pay the telephone tax is punishable under IRC § 7203 with a $10,000 fine or one year in jail or both. There are no known cases of prosecution for failure to pay this tax, but such refusals are a relatively recent development and the law in this area remains unclear as to the consequences of refusal.

If you should withhold your telephone tax, enclose a note with your payment indicating that you are paying the phone bill but not the tax.

C. *Non-criminal Consequences of Failure to Pay Federal Taxes*

Sooner or later, the IRS will probably try to collect any unpaid taxes. Collections are typically made in the easiest possible way. The service will first try to deduct the amount owed from pending tax refunds. Then, in the following order, it will attempt to seize bank accounts, wages, and personal property (IRC § 6331). Clothes, school books and some household and business equipment are, however, exempt from seizure (IRC § 6334).

In addition to the tax itself, 6% interest per year and a penalty tax are added. The penalty tax is 5% of the underpayment in the case of negligence or intentional disregard of the rules (IRC § 6653(a)) and 50% of the underpayment in the case of fraud (IRC § 6653(b)). Tax resistance would most probably be treated as intentional disregard with the 5% penalty imposed—provided you file a return. Again, the IRS seems to prefer this method of collection rather than criminal sanctions, but civil collection, civil penalties and criminal penalties are not mutually exclusive and it is conceivable that all may be applied.

CHAPTER TWO

RESTRICTIONS ON POLITICAL ACTIVITY

Chapter One attempted to explain the rights which the normal citizen has when he engages in political activity. However, there are some situations in which the rights of certain classes of individuals, such as government employees, school teachers, students and military personnel are closely restricted and regulated. It is the purpose of this chapter to explain these restrictions. In general, if you have any doubts or questions as to whether or not your rights have been restricted due to your occupation and/or status, then you should consult the authorities, your employer, etc., who should be aware of such restrictions and request a clear statement of your rights. If the restrictions as presented seem unduly harsh, it would be wise to consult a lawyer as to their possible unconstitutionality before undertaking any action in violation thereof.

I. Private Employees

Employees in private companies and firms have few legal protections. A private employer may generally hire and fire, promote and demote and discipline his employees as he sees fit. Nevertheless, in certain situations, an employee who engages in some forms of political activity may be protected. This protection can come from any of three sources.

First, if you have a private employment contract, read it to see what rights and obligations you and your employer have. Contracts differ from job to job. Your contract may specify that employment will continue for a certain period or even indefinitely, as long as your work is satisfactory. If you have such a contract and you continue to perform satisfactory work, you should not be subject to discharge or discipline. Discharge or discipline for political activity that does not take place at work or during working hours is clearly a breach of such a private employment contract and you can sue your employer. If, however, the political activity results in some significant disruption of your employer's business, such as an unexcused absence from work to engage in a peaceful demonstration, then he may claim that your work is not satisfactory since you are not performing work as requested. Under such circumstances a discharge or disciplinary action may be justified because it is the employee who has first breached the employment contract. The less inconvenience your political activity causes your employer, the weaker his justification for discharge or discipline.

Nonetheless, it is important to remember that in the private employment situation, the private employer has the initiative and only through court action—a long, tedious and expensive process—can the employee gain redress. Even if you win, you will usually only get money damages, since the court will rarely order an employer to take back an employee.

Second, if you are a union member, you are covered under a union contract with your employer. Read the labor agreement to see what are your protections and rights. Generally, an employee can only be disciplined or discharged for "just cause." Just cause

may be defined in the labor agreement, and may include absence from work without valid excuse. In the absence of express language, one day's absence might or might not be grounds for discharge. Discharge for one day's absence is a rather harsh action. Federal statutes state that the union is under a duty to fairly represent union members who have been discriminated against by an employer. Therefore, if you have been unfairly disciplined or discharged, the union must take some action to protect you. If your union is strong and sympathetic, then this protection may be significant. But it is again important to remember that the employer acts first, and then the union reacts. The union grievance procedure may also be long and tedious and perhaps inconclusive.

Third, private employees are given certain limited protections by California statutes, as is the case in nearly every state. California Labor Code sections 1101-1105 protect certain political activities from employer reprisals.

Section 1101 states:

No employer shall make, adopt, or enforce any rule, regulation, or policy: (a) Forbidding or preventing employees from engaging or participating in politics or from becoming candidates for public office. (b) Controlling or directing, or tending to control or direct the political activities or affiliations of employees.

Section 1102 states:

No employer shall coerce or influence or attempt to coerce or influence his employees through or by means of threat to discharge or loss of employment to adopt or follow or refrain from adopting or following any particular course or line of political action or political activity.

Violation of these statutes is a crime and also gives you a chance to sue for damages.

These statutes have not been used much in California, but the language is very broad and the courts have interpreted political activity to mean more than partisan politics during elections. The statutes certainly seem to protect an employee from retaliation by his employer for political activity that does not affect the employer's business. Therefore, an employer may not fire an employee because the employee participated in a peace march on Sunday afternoon, a non-work day. If the political activity amounts to a significant disruption of the employer's business, then the Labor Code sections may offer less protection. But these California statutes are very liberal and may well protect all sorts of political activity. Show these sections to your employer. He may be persuaded to work out some accommodation for your activities.

The private employer is mainly concerned with getting his work done. He knows that good employees are hard to find. He might, therefore, be willing to make some concessions. If you have a union which supports your position, or significant numbers of your fellow employees support you, then your position is much stronger. If public opinion is behind your activity, your position is also stronger.

A number of compromises which protect your job and yet conform to your employer's normal procedures may be worked out. He may be willing to grant you a leave without pay (employers do not have to pay wages when no work is performed), or you may be able to take your annual leave, or, if your contract provides it, a floating holiday. Before you take any action, check with your contract, your union or your employer to see what mechanisms are available to you. Most of these procedures require advance notice to and consent of your employer.

II. Public Employees

The following materials discuss a highly complex and sensitive area, that of the political rights of public employees. This analysis of federal civil service regulations is general in nature, and does not examine what limitations may be additionally imposed upon your activity, should you be employed in a sensitive security position; nor does the subsection cover the issue of membership in political organizations. As to the latter, membership in an organization deemed subversive by the Attorney General may very well cost you your job; it may also subject you to criminal prosecution. At this time all the editor can suggest is, be certain of what the goals and policies are of every group with which you might associate yourself politically, and if you do have trouble along these lines, contact your nearest American Civil Liberties Union office.

The analysis of state and local civil service regulations, as well as the materials which follow regarding the rights and freedoms of students, faculty and staff at colleges, universities and high schools, are all couched in terms of Federal and California decisions and statutes. Whenever the case material cited is U.S., rely on it as the law controlling your rights. In the other areas where relevant California statutory sections are cited as controlling, your own state laws, or academic rules and regulations might be quite divergent, or even contradictory. While it might be nice if the literal law were the law of the land ("Congress shall make no law . . . abridging the freedom of speech"), the reality is otherwise. Before acting in an area that is designated by a California statute in the text below, it would be well to check the corresponding provisions in your own state.

GOVERNMENT EMPLOYEES

A. *Government Employees*

1. *Federal Civil Service.* Federal employees' right to engage in political activity is regulated by the *Hatch Act,* 5 U.S.C. 7321 *et seq.* The act *forbids* you to solicit among yourselves for political purposes, use official authority or influence to interfere with or affect the result of an election, or actively participate in political management or in political campaigns. The act *permits* you to vote as you choose, express opinions on political subjects and candidates (including letter-writing to newspapers), and participate in *nonpartisan* political activities such as constitutional amendments, referendums, approval of municipal ordinances and similar activities which are not specifically identified with a national or state political party. The Civil Service Commission has declared that federal employees are generally free to express their political opinions publicly, to display political buttons, badges and automobile stickers, to join political organizations and participate as members of such organizations, and to attend political meetings, rallies and fund-raising functions during off-duty hours (Civil Service Commission Pamphlet on Political Activities). The penalty for violation of the *Hatch Act* is dismissal unless the Civil Service Commission unanimously agrees that the violation does not warrant dismissal, in which case a penalty of not less than 30 days suspension without pay is imposed.

Public employees cannot be fired for exercising their constitutional rights. Under the Federal statute, however, you can be discharged or suspended without pay for just cause if it will promote the efficiency of the public service, 5 U.S.C. § 7501. This means that if your political activity interferes with the orderly performance of the service, you may be discharged or suspended. (For example, postal workers may not distribute leaflets to customers during working hours because this activity disturbs the orderly performance of postal service.) Public employees can, however, engage in such political activities as holding a peaceful demonstration during off-duty hours or displaying resolutions on bulletin boards.

Public employees do not have the right to strike for economic or any other reasons. Political activities during working hours will be treated as absence from work without leave, and will be treated as any other absence without leave. There are no legal protections for such absences, although employees are entitled to prior notice and a hearing. Employees who wish to take time off to engage in political activities should therefore look into the possibility of taking a leave without pay or a holiday if they do not wish to risk losing their jobs.

2. State and Local Civil Service. The right of state employees to engage in political activity is regulated by the CAL GOVERNMENT CODE. Those political activities which the Code says you may not engage in are: soliciting or receiving contributions for political purposes; allowing others to solicit or receive contributions in government places under your control; using your official authority or influence to coerce votes or political action; and any other activities which can be necessarily implied as prohibited from the above prohibitions, CAL GOVERNMENT CODE § § 19730-19739.

All officers and employees of a local agency (county, city, city and county, political subdivision, district, or municipal corporation) are subject to the regulations of CAL GOVERNMENT CODE § § 3201-3206. Under these provisions, local officers and employees are similarly prohibited from those activities mentioned above with respect to state employees. Furthermore, these provisions clearly provide that no local employee shall participate in political activities of any kind while he is in uniform, and that no local employee shall take an active part in any campaign. (School district employees are not subject to the regulations mentioned above. Their activities are regulated by the Education Code (see 2(b)(2) below).)

Those state and local employees whose services are financially supported by federal funds are subject to the *Hatch Act*. Such employees are mainly those who work for public health, public welfare, housing, urban renewal, area development, unemployment compensation, highways and civil defense. The provisions of the *Hatch Act* are discussed in part (a) of this section.

State and local employees may be disciplined for a number of causes, CAL GOVERNMENT CODE § 19572. Several of these may become relevant when you become a political protester. (1) "Improper political activity" is a cause for disciplinary action. The term is vague, but it seems safe to say that traditional free speech activities such as those outlined in Chapter I above, if carried on during off-duty hours, are not "improper." In fact, they are protected by both the U.S. and California Constitutions. (2) "Misuse of state property" is another cause for disciplinary action. This means, for example, that you cannot legally place partisan political literature in your office waiting room, solicit campaign contributions or hold a "sit-in" on the premises. (3) Strikes by public employees are illegal, and picketing can be enjoined. If you become involved in such activities, whether your purpose is economic or political, your absence from work may be treated as "inexcusable absence without leave," which is another cause for discipline. (4) Finally there is a catch-all provision which says that you may be disciplined for "other failure of good behavior either during or outside of duty hours which is of such a nature that it causes discredit to (your) agency or (your) employment." So far, this clause appears to have been used primarily to discipline employees who engage in such practices as fixing traffic tickets. If, however, your employer uses it to punish you for peaceful, legal speech activities, the courts will almost certainly declare his action unconstitutional.

Your agency may have other rules and regulations governing your political activity. Before you do anything, find out what those regulations are. If they seem excessively restrictive (if, for example, they deny you the right to participate in traditional political and speech activities during your free time), ask a lawyer what to do. You may be able to get the agency to liberalize its rules so that you can engage in your intended activity.

B. *Employees of Educational Institutions*

1. U. C. Employees. University employees, academic and non-academic, are members of the University community, and as such are subject to University and campus rules regarding on-campus conduct and use of University facilities. The section on U.C. students discusses in greater detail the rules and regulations which apply to both students and employees.

University employees are not subject to the civil service laws of this state, CAL CONSTITUTION Article 24, § 4. The special rules governing University employees are to be found in various publications of the University.

a. *Academic Employees.* The University respects the academic freedom of faculty to engage in political activity that does not interfere with the performance of their duties. Violations of this freedom are investigated by the Academic Freedom Committee of the Academic Senate, UNIVERSITY OF CALIFORNIA, MANUAL OF THE ACADEMIC SENATE By-Law 90 (hereafter referred to as SENATE).

Faculty members can be disciplined by the University for "good cause." Proceedings for dismissal, suspension, or demotion of faculty members are conducted by the Divisional Committee on Privilege and Tenure. You are entitled to a written complaint which is to be filed with the Committee, notice, a full and fair hearing, a record of the proceedings and other procedural safeguards, SENATE BY-LAW 112 (c).

In 1966, the Regents passed a resolution stating that professors and instructors who went on strike or refused to meet their classes would be subject to dismissal. This resolution apparently has never been repealed. The legality and effect of this resolution is an open question.

If you want to take time off from your normal duties to engage in political activity, you should consider applying for a leave of absence. Leaves of absence with pay can be granted to academic employees for "good cause," UNIVERSITY OF CALIFORNIA, ADMINISTRATIVE MANUAL § 176-0. The Chancellor can authorize paid leaves for up to 30 days; longer ones require the President's recommendation and the Regents' approval, ADMINISTRATIVE MANUAL § 176-24. The Chancellor can also authorize leaves of absence without pay for "good cause" for up to one year; such leaves cannot extend beyond June 30 of the academic year for which they are granted, ADMINISTRATIVE MANUAL § § 176-0, 176-24. To apply for either kind of leave, you need to ask for and fill out a standard application form (Form 1510 for leaves with pay, Form 1602 for leaves without pay).

b. *Non-academic Employees.* Disciplinary action may be taken against non-academic employees "because of inattention to duty, inefficiency, insubordination, absence without permission, violation of law or University regulations, intemperance, dishonesty, misuse of public funds or property, or other misconduct which adversely affects the university, UNIVERSITY OF CALIFORNIA, PERSONNEL RULES FOR STAFF

[45]

EMPLOYEES Rule 25.1 (hereafter referred to as PER-SONNEL). You may be subject to anything from a written warning, a mandatory making up of time (for unauthorized absences), to a salary reduction, reassignment, demotion, suspension without pay or dismissal. Generally, disciplinary actions other than make-up time entitle you to at least one written warning, PERSONNEL RULES 25.2, 25.4. Procedures for appeals are set out in PERSONNEL RULE 26.

The activities of employee organizations may be subject to special regulations on each campus. To learn what these rules are on your campus, consult the Personnel Office.

If you want time off to participate in political activities, consider applying for a leave of absence. "Employees may be granted leaves of absence" to do work "in the interest of public service," PERSONNEL Rule 18.1. Leaves without pay can be granted for up to six months by department chairmen; a Chancellor, Vice President, or University Dean can grant leaves for up to 12 months, PERSONNEL Rules 18.1-.2. Although you won't be paid for such leaves, neither will you lose your job. If you call in sick, you will get paid, but you run the risk of being disciplined if your department finds out that you were not really sick.

PERSONNEL Rule 14.2.F provides: "An employee may be granted time off [with pay] during a public emergency, as designated by the Chancellor, which effectively prevents his attendance at work or the continuance of work in a normal and orderly manner." "Public emergency" is defined to include riots, demonstrations, and sabotage. It is not clear whether the Chancellor need only designate the state of emergency for department heads to grant you time off, or whether the Chancellor himself must authorize the time off.

2. California State College Employees. State College employees, academic and non-academic alike, are

subject to dismissal, suspension or demotion for immoral or unprofessional conduct, incompetency, or failure to perform official duties, CAL EDUCATION CODE § 24306. You may also be disciplined for disruption or attempted disruption, by force and violence, of instruction, recruiting or any other authorized activity of the college, CAL ADMINISTRATIVE CODE § 43526. While you are not subject to the state civil service laws, CAL CONSTITUTION art. 24, § 4, you *are* entitled to a hearing on your dismissal, suspension or demotion before the State Personnel Board if you request one, CAL EDUCATION CODE § 24309-10.

3. Community or Junior College Employees
a. *Academic Employees.* As long as you do not advocate the violent overthrow of the government, your political activities during your off-hours are your own business and the school may not regulate them, EDUCATION CODE § 13004. You are a bit less free at school. For the most part, you are subject to the same kinds of rules and regulations as high school teachers (see (4) below), though it is likely that you will in fact be permitted to express yourself on political issues more freely because your students are theoretically more mature and less impressionable than high school students. In one important area, this greater freedom is made explicit in the law. The Education Code *forbids* high school teachers to "propagandize" their students on school premises by bulletins, circulars, etc. You *are allowed* to "propagandize" as long as your activity does not "impede the orderly conduct of school classes and programs." You must, however, follow the board's rules and regulations governing such activity (these will be rules about the times, places, and ways in which you may engage in activity). The board does have power to forbid you to distribute material advocating unlawful acts. If you plan to distribute such

literature, you should check with your particular board to see if they have such a rule. If they do, you will have to decide whether to risk disciplinary proceedings for illegal political activity.

i. Disciplinary Proceedings. If you engage in political expression you may run afoul of school officials who will attempt to suspend or dismiss you; they may also seek to revoke your teaching credential. However, if they choose to do so, they must follow strict procedures which limit the grounds for dismissal and require that you be given time to defend yourself. These particular rules apply equally to high school teachers as well. A *permanent teacher* may only be dismissed for one of the following reasons: (1) Immoral or unprofessional conduct, (2) Commission, aiding, or advocating acts of "criminal syndicalism," (3) Dishonesty, (4) Incompetency, (5) Physical or mental condition making you unfit to instruct or associate with children, (6) Persistent violation of or refusal to obey school laws of the State or reasonable rules of the board of the governing school district, (7) Conviction of a felony or of a crime of "moral turpitude," (8) Any of a number of activities associated with communism.

Before formally dismissing any permanent academic employee, the governing school board must give you full notice of all charges against you. The board can only act if someone files written charges against you. It can then decide to notify you that unless you request a hearing to defend yourself, you will be dismissed after 30 days. If you do request a hearing, and the board still wants to suspend you, then (since you are a permanent employee) the board must file a complaint against you in a California Superior Court. The court will then decide whether the board has sufficient grounds for the suspension. The board can never send a teacher a notice of intention to dismiss during the summer months—May 15 to September 15.

There are several additions and exceptions to these rules. If the board wishes to dismiss a permanent teacher for the specific reason of incompetency or unprofessional conduct, then it must give him notice of the precise and detailed charges against him and at least a 90-day period to correct his deficiencies. Only after it has done so may the board give him the required 30 day notice of intention to dismiss. If the charges against the teacher are either immoral conduct, conviction of a felony or a crime of "moral turpitude," incompetency due to mental illness, or for various specified communist activities, the board may suspend the teacher at the same time it gives him the 30-day notice of intention to dismiss, EDUCATION CODE § § 13403-441. During the actual school year, the rights of *probationary teachers* are the same as those of permanent teachers. During the school year a school board may only dismiss you for the same causes and with the same procedures as for dismissal of a permanent teacher. However, at the conclusion of any school year, the governing school board may give you notice that you will not be rehired for the coming year.

A board that wishes to give notice to a probationary employee is subject to certain restrictions and must follow definite procedures. It may only dismiss you for deficiencies which relate to the welfare of the school or its pupils. No later than March 15 the school superintendent must notify both you and the governing school board that the superintendent recommends against rehiring. The superintendent must state his reasons. You then have at least seven days to request a hearing to determine if the board has cause not to rehire you. If you request a hearing, the board must hold one on or before April 15. You have at least five days to prepare answers to the charges against you. If the board decides not to rehire the teacher, it must give him notice that he will not be rehired by May 15. If it fails to do so, the teacher is automatically rehired for the coming academic year. (A substitute teacher is not considered a probationary teacher and can be dismissed at any time, without cause, EDUCATION CODE § § 13442-445.)

ii. Suspension or Revocation of Credential. Whenever at the local level a teacher is charged with immoral or unprofessional conduct or evident unfitness for service or persistent defiance of the laws regulating the duties of his position, the State Board of Education may direct that the county board of education hold a hearing on the charges and recommend whether or not the State Board should suspend or revoke the teacher's credential. You are entitled to notice and a hearing in accordance with standard California procedure.

A county board may also suspend or revoke a credential for the above reasons. The original charges against you must be made to the board in writing under oath, the teacher must be given at least 10 days to prepare for the hearing, and he may be represented by legal counsel, EDUCATION CODE § § 13202-214.

b. *Non-academic Employees.* Section 13004 of the Education Code discussed above covers non-academic employees as well. You have a right to engage in political activities during your off-duty hours, short of advocating the violent overthrow of the government. Education Code Section 13752 provides that you may not engage in political activities during your assigned hours of employment but that you may not be demoted or removed or discriminated against in any way because of political acts, opinions or affiliations.

4. Secondary School Teachers

a. *Public.* During off-duty hours, public school teachers may participate fully and freely in political activities, CAL EDUCATION CODE § 13004.

The Education Code prohibits legislative bodies and school districts from regulating such activities with the single exception of advocating violent overthrow of the government.

General Rights. During school hours, you have all the rights to engage in political activity which have been outlined in Chapter One above, *except* insofar as the "special characteristics of the school environment" justify greater restrictions. Courts require schools to show "a compelling state interest" before allowing them to restrict your First Amendment rights and even when allowing your rights to be restricted, the Courts require that the school pick the least burdensome means of doing so.

Hopefully, you won't have to go to court to preserve your rights. While school officials will always be able to give reasons for their rules, you may be able to convince them that the reasons are not "compelling" ones. The general principles by which the balancing of your interests as a teacher and those of the school and government must be made have recently been delineated by both the U.S. and California Supreme Courts. The language of these cases may be useful in assessing what your rights are as teachers and may aid you in convincing your principal or superintendent that certain political activities should be allowed (note that the language of these cases applies equally to your students' rights).

The government has no valid interest in restricting or prohibiting speech or speech-related activity simply in order to avert the sort of disturbance, argument or unrest which is inevitably generated by the expression of ideas which are controversial and invite dispute. The danger justifying restriction or prohibition must be one which "rises far above public inconvenience, annoyance or unrest." (*Terminello,* p. 4).

"Any word spoken, in class, in the lunchroom or on the campus, that deviates from the views of another person, may start an argument or cause a disturbance. But our Constitution says we must take this risk . . ." (*Tinker v. Des Moines School District* 393 U.S. 503, 508, 1969). School officials must produce "facts which might reasonably have led [them] to forecast *substantial disruption of or material interference with school activities."* (*Tinker,* p. 514). Similarly, in order to justify a restraint on the political activities of teachers, such officials must demonstrate that the restraint is a practical necessity in order to meet a "compelling public need to protect the efficiency and integrity of the public service." *Los Angeles Teachers Union v. L.A. City Bd. of Ed.* 78 Cal. Rptr., 723, 728 (1969).

The rights of students and teachers to express their views on school policies and governmental actions relating to schools and the power of school authorities to regulate political activities of students and faculty, are of peculiar concern to our state and nation today. Education is in a state of ferment, if not turmoil. When controversies arising from or contributing to this turbulence are brought before the courts, it is imperative that the courts carefully differentiate in treatment those who are violent and heedless of the rights of others as they assert their cause and those whose concerns are no less burning but who seek to express themselves through peaceful, orderly means. In order to discourage persons from engaging in the former type of activity, the courts must take pains to assure that the channels of peaceful communication remain open and that peaceful activity is fully protected. (*L.A. Teachers,* p. 732.)

Although many activities have not been ruled upon by the courts and will have to be judged by the general language set forth above, some activities are clearly permitted and constitutionally protected.

Wearing of arm bands to protest the war and the draft. Although *Tinker,* above, held only that students can wear such arm bands, there was very strong language in that case which makes it clear that teachers can also wear armbands. In order to justify a prohibition on armbands, your school would have to show that there would be serious disruption of the school if armbands were worn.

Letters to a newspaper criticizing the school board. Teachers may not be dismissed for writing critical letters to newspapers unless by so doing they interfere with the efficient operation of the school sufficiently to justify dismissal. Even false statements do not justify dismissal unless proof is offered that they are knowingly false or recklessly made. Statements on issues of public concern which neither interfere with a teacher's teaching duties nor with the school's general operation are entitled to the same protection as if they had been made by a member of the general public, *Pickering v. Board of Education,* 391 U.S. 563 (1968).

Circulation of petitions among teachers. Teachers have the right to circulate petitions among their colleagues during duty-free lunch periods at the school (*L.A. Teachers Union* above).

Any activities during off-duty hours short of advocating violent overthrow. Section 13004 of the Education Code, cited in *Los Angeles Teachers Union,* above, unequivocally establishes this right to engage in political activities during off-duty hours.

There are several trouble areas where the law is unclear. Older cases gave a very restrictive reading to a teacher's constitutional rights. These cases have been nullified or at least seriously weakened by the development in the last few years of First Amendment rights, but they leave some doubts.

Supporting particular candidates in class. One of these older cases upheld the dismissal of a teacher for "unprofessional conduct" for advocating in class the election of a particular candidate for county supervisor of schools, *Goldsmith v. The Board of Education of Sacramento City High School District,* 66 Cal. App. 157 (1924). The case has not been overruled and may have continued vitality.

Solicitation of funds or membership. EDUCATION CODE § 9021 expressly prohibits solicitation of funds or memberships from students by teachers on the school premises.

Circulating a petition among students. This may be treated by courts in the same manner as advocating election of candidates was treated in *Goldsmith,* and solicitation of funds from students is treated under EDUCATION CODE § 9013. The rationale behind all of these rules is that high school students are sufficiently impressionable and high school teachers sufficiently influential with their students that they can unduly influence students to accept certain political beliefs, sign petitions or donate funds.

Propagandizing or soliciting for membership. EDUCATION CODE § 9013 prohibits proselytizing activity by all persons from one hour before until one hour after school is out. This is clearly broader than the constitution will permit. *Los Angeles Teachers Union* explicitly held that some activity this statute purports to prohibit is permissible (circulation among faculty of a petition during duty free lunch periods) and recent cases have exempted some student activity from its prohibitions as well (see section on high school students, below). How much is left of the statute is unclear. It is unlikely, however, that courts would be inclined to protect propagandizing of high school students by faculty in the classroom.

Code of Ethics for Teachers. The California State Board of Education has just adopted a code of ethics for the teaching profession, Cal. Administrative Code § 5480 *et seq.* It is of interest because it purports to give more explicit meaning to the term "unprofessional conduct," ED. CODE § 13202 and § 13403, which if serious enough is a ground for dismissal. There may be some question about the validity of these rules, but for now assume that they are valid. They specify that you are neither to use your position for personal financial gain by exploiting either students or parents or by taking bribes, nor may you discriminate on the basis of race, color, creed or national origin. The code also specifies that it is your duty as a teacher to provide access to varying points of view (sec. 5481 (a)) and that you should give all points of view a fair hearing (sec. 5481 (b)). Most importantly, section 5484 provides that *only the following* constitute unprofessional conduct amounting to cause for suspension, revocation, or denial of a certification document, or renewal: violations which involve jeopardy to student welfare, which evidence malice, serious incompetency or bad judgment, or which show a consistent pattern of misconduct.

Your political activities could get you in trouble with school authorities. There may come a time when, for political or moral reasons, you feel you have to go beyond the bounds of the rules and laws, either to test and change them or because you believe civil disobedience is justified. As a result, you may face demotion, suspension or dismissal or even revocation of your credential. You have certain rights to notice and a hearing. These are discussed on p. 48 above, since junior college teachers are subject to the same rules.

b. *Private.* Private high school teachers do not presently have the on-campus constitutional protections that public high school teachers do. If you are willing to go to court, there is some chance that the court would grant you some rights (your lawyer would argue that private schools perform a "public function" and that the state, because it makes certain rules governing private schools, is sufficiently involved in private schools that what takes place in them is "state action"). If you are not willing to go to court or do not have the time and money, your strength is in persuasion and organization. Get your fellow teachers together, plan constructive, non-disruptive activities, and go to your school authorities armed with unanimity and reason.

c. *High School Non-academic Employees.* Your rights are the same as junior college non-academic employees. See p. 50.

Bibliography for Teachers:
W. Murphy, Academic Freedom—An Emerging Constitutional Right, 28 Law and Contemporary Problems 445 (1963).
For University Professors:
T. Emerson & D. Haber, Academic Freedom of the Faculty Member as Citizen, 28 Law and Contemporary Problems 525 (1963).

III. Students

First Amendment rights to freedom of speech are available to students. "It can hardly be argued that either students or teachers shed their constitutional rights to freedom of speech or expression at the schoolhouse gate," *Tinker v. Des Moines School District,* 393 U.S. 503, 506 (1969).

The right to freedom of speech includes such political activity as passing out leaflets and handbills, wearing buttons, armbands, etc., holding student assemblies, and other similar activities. The protection of these activities provided by the First Amendment, however, is *not* unlimited. A great deal of student political activity is *not* regarded by the courts as protected by the First Amendment. The courts take the position that regulations limiting the exercise of free speech are constitutional when justified by valid school interests, such as the maintenance of order and tranquility.

The test used to determine whether speech activities of students are constitutionally protected, as set forth in the recent Supreme Court decision of *Tinker v. Des Moines School District,* above, is that students are free to express themselves so long as there is no indication that such expression would *"materially and substantially interfere with the requirements of appropriate discipline in the operation of the school."* An alternative formulation of this test was set forth in the recent California case of *Myers v. Arcata Union High School District,* 269 C.A. 2d 549 (1969). The court in that case said that in order for the constitutional rights of students to be restricted, three requirements must be met: 1) the restriction imposed must rationally relate to the enhancement of the educational function, 2) the benefit gained by the public must outweigh the resulting impairment of the students' rights, and 3) there can be no alternative less subversive of the students' constitutional rights.

The application of this test can result in different outcomes in different situations. The courts have held that the power of the state (and of the schools) to limit the constitutional freedoms of children is greater than its power to limit the constitutional freedoms of adults. Hence, school authorities need less legal support to justify regulation of high school students than they need to justify regulation of college or university students. For instance, California courts have held that a high school can prohibit the wearing of beards or long hair by high school students on the ground that it is likely to result in disruption or distraction. It is very doubtful that the courts would permit a college or university to enforce similar regulations. Likewise, political activity that might be considered disruptive in a high school context might not be considered disruptive in a university context. Even in the university, however, activity such as disrupting classes, blocking doorways and hallways, unauthorized use of loudspeakers, etc., is not constitutionally protected.

The basic principle is that students have a right to express themselves and to engage in political activity where such expression and action does not interfere with the normal functioning of the school. It is not always altogether clear just how this principle will be applied. Students can be constitutionally required to comply with school regulations regarding the time, place, and manner of assemblies, and to refrain from disruptive activities. But they cannot be totally foreclosed from the exercise of First Amendment rights, and the school must have a legitimate interest to protect in order to restrict the exercise of those rights.

A. *University of California Students*

1. Rights and Regulations. You have a right, along with other members of the University community, to participate in peaceful expression and advocacy on campus, including political expression and advocacy, UNIVERSITY POLICIES, pp. 6, 10. Such activity may include speeches, public meetings, and the distribution and posting of literature (such literature *must* state the name of the person or registered student organization on whose behalf it is distributed). You must conduct these activities, however, according to the time, place, and manner regulations of your particular campus. Typical campus regulations designate the areas where such activities may take place, provide procedures for reserving campus facilities, control the use of outdoor tables, and regulate the use of sound amplification equipment.

Your protest activity may assume a form that will go contrary to University or campus regulations, and if you engage in disruptive conduct on campus, such as obstruction of University activities (teaching, research, etc.), physical abuse or vandalism, or "disorderly conduct or lewd, indecent, or obscene conduct or expression," or violate University or campus regulations, you are subject to University disciplinary proceedings, UNIVERSITY POLICIES, p. 5. As a result, you may be warned, censured, put on probation, suspended, dismissed, or even expelled, UNIVERSITY POLICIES, pp. 12-13. Moreover, if you use university facilities for organizing or carrying out unlawful activity, you may be subject both to disciplinary action by the university and prosecution by the state.

During periods of campus emergency, as designated by the chancellor, emergency regulations may be substituted for the usual regulations governing the time, place and manner of public expression, UNIVERSITY POLICIES, p. 4. In such a situation, most of your normal rights disappear and you can be disciplined for trying to exercise them. Typically, during a state of emergency, public assembly, use of sound amplification and use of university facilities for political purposes are all forbidden.

Your off-campus conduct is not subject to University discipline "unless such conduct affects (your) suitability as a student," UNIVERSITY POLICIES, p. 9.

2. Classes, Exams and Grades. In times of political emergency, you may want to give up class attendance to engage in political activities. There are no University regulations requiring class attendance. However, professors and instructors are free to consider class attendance in determining your grade. If you plan to miss class, it might make sense to ask each of your instructors for his policy on class attendance.

University regulations are more explicit as to final examinations: "No student shall be excused from assigned final examinations," UNIVERSITY OF CALIFORNIA, MANUAL OF THE ACADEMIC SENATE, Regulation 770 (hereafter referred to as SENATE). The only exception to this rule is that degree candidates may elect to be examined in their major field rather than their specific courses in the quarter they expect to earn their degree, SENATE, Regulation 772(D). Final exams are required to be assigned in all undergraduate courses (other than laboratories) unless special dispensation is received from the Committee on Courses on the recommendation of the department chairman, SENATE, Regulation 772 (A)-(C).

Although it is probably rare, a professor may express his distaste for your political activities by giving you a lower grade than you deserve. In such a situation you have three possible recourses.

Informal. First, try to persuade the professor into giving you the grade you deserve. Tell him you are going to talk to the head of the department or the dean of the college or school. If he doesn't correct the grade, do so. If they believe your story they may be able to convince him to change the grade.

Formal. If you can't get redress through informal means, you have two possible courses open to you.

If you get an "F" grade, the academic senate committee governing courses on your campus may have the power to override it. On the Berkeley campus, the Academic Senate Committee on Courses has the power to override "F's" and substitute a grade of "passed," *Manual of the Academic Senate,* p. 66, Reg. A206. To challenge an "F" on the Berkeley campus, you must file a petition showing that the instructor used factors other than achievement and proficiency in the subject matter to determine your grade. If you make a good case, the Committee on Courses will request an investigation of the dean of the college or school in which the course was given. The dean is required to provide a fair proceeding for both instructor and student and must report his findings and recommendation to the Committee on Courses. Both you and the instructor will receive copies of the dean's report and you may submit written comments to the Committee before final decision.

A "Not Passed" grade may be challenged by this procedure only if you can show that the grade is the equivalent of an "F." Since "Not Passed" may be equivalent to either "D" or "F," you may have a hard time establishing that the grade was equivalent to "F."

If you didn't get an "F," and have good proof and lots of time and money, you may be able to challenge the grade in court.

If, of course, a grade reflects only the instructor's evaluation of your achievement, a court will not question his judgment, *Miller v. Dailey,* 136 Cal. 212, 68 P. 1029 (1902). If you receive a low grade as punishment for behavior which is not related to your work in class, the court will examine your case to see whether school officials can properly prohibit that behavior. Many kinds of protest activity are protected by the First Amendment and cannot be prohibited by the school. When courts have found such action unreasonable, they have ordered school officials to grant diplomas which the officials have refused on the basis of a student's behavior out of class, *Valentine v. Independent School District,* 174 N.W. 334. If the grade is actually imposed as punishment, due process may require notice and hearing, *Dixon v. Alabama State Board of Education,* 294 F. 2d 150 (1961); *Goldberg v. Regents of the University of California,* 248 Cal. App. 2d 867, 57 Cal. Rptr. 463 (1967).

3. Student Organizations. Student groups wishing to engage in political activities on University campuses should consider becoming registered student organiza-

tions. Registered student organizations can engage in two types of on-campus activities that individual students or unregistered student groups cannot. First, as a member of a registered organization you can solicit funds (although the Chancellor may permit fund solicitation by specified charitable organizations, public service agencies, and University or University-related groups as well). Second, you can invite non-University speakers to the campus with the approval of the Chancellor. Finally, you will have an easier time reserving University facilities than do student groups which aren't registered, UNIVERSITY POLICIES, pp. 7, 10.

Any organization whose active membership is limited to students and other University personnel can become a registered student organization by complying with campus registration procedures, UNIVERSITY POLICIES, p. 6. These procedures typically require filing a list of the organization's officers, a statement of its purpose, a copy of its bylaws, and other similar information. If your organization violates University and campus rules, your registration may be revoked, UNIVERSITY POLICIES, p. 7.

B. *California State College Students*

Students (and other members of the campus community) may hold meetings and rallies and distribute non-commercial literature on state college campuses. While solicitation of funds is not specifically mentioned, the regulations permit sale of newspapers, magazines, pamphlets, etc., that are not available at the college bookstore as long as they are not obscene, 5 CAL. ADMINISTRATIVE CODE § § 42351-42353. The individual campuses have further rules governing the time, place and manner of such activities. Typical campus regulations permit student organizations to invite speakers onto the campus and use college facilities and allow demonstrations that do not obstruct classes or cause inconvenience on campus.

You can be disciplined for a long list of offenses, a number of which become relevant when you get involved in campus political demonstrations. These are: obstruction or disruption, *on or off college property,* of the state college educational or administrative process or other college functions; physical abuse, *on or off college property,* of the person or property of any member of the college community or members of his family, or even the threat of such physical abuse; theft of, or non-accidental damage to, state college property or property in the possession of or owned by a member of the college community (you can be required to pay for such property and the college has the power to withhold your grades or diploma until you do so); unauthorized entry into or use or misuse of state college property; possession of or use of explosives, dangerous chemicals, or deadly weapons on state college property or at state college functions without the prior authorization of the president; lewd, indecent or obscene behavior; abusive behavior directed toward a member of the college community; violation of an order of the state college president of which you have notice; and, finally, soliciting or assisting another to do any of the above acts, 5 CAL ADMINISTRATIVE CODE § 41301. Further, if you violate or even attempt to violate the trustee's rules and regulations for the government and maintenance of the buildings and grounds, the Education Code provides that you are guilty of a misdemeanor, ED. CODE § 23604.1.

Finally, during a campus emergency, the President apparently has the power to suspend your free speech rights by promulgating emergency regulations. During such an emergency, he also has the power to give interim suspensions if he thinks you are likely to repeat your "offense." He is, however, required to give notice and a hearing within a week after suspending you.

C. *Community or Junior College Students*

At present, there is only one state-wide rule governing free speech activities on junior college campuses. That rule says that student political organizations affiliated with the official youth division of any political party on the ballot in California may hold meetings on campus and distribute bulletins and circulars concerning its meetings provided school authorities do not endorse the organization and its activities do not interfere with the regular education program. If the activity described in this provision is meant to be the *only* political activity that can take place on campus, it is unconstitutionally restrictive. Your rights should parallel the rights of university and college students (see the two preceding sections). A student code of conduct, which has already been approved by the Peralta Colleges and is being considered by the other junior college districts in the state, will presumably go into effect for fall 1970. It should cover student political activity. In the meantime, check with your district to find out what rules, if any, govern your speech and political activity.

D. *Secondary School Students*

1. Public. For many years, courts almost never interfered with the discretion of high school authorities in matters of student conduct and discipline. The rights of high school students to express themselves on political issues were largely ignored. There are some indications that this traditional attitude of the courts has undergone some change in recent years, specifically in the area of student First Amendment rights to free speech. Before looking further into what your First Amendment rights are, however, we will look at the general outlines of the regulation of student conduct.

Student Conduct and Discipline

You are subject to disciplinary sanctions, including suspension or, in some cases, expulsion, for violations of various statutory rules or local school regulations. The following are examples of statutory violations: (1) continued willful disobedience, (2) open and persistent defiance of the authority of school personnel, (3) abuse of school personnel, (4) other obvious offenses such as assault and battery upon students or school personnel, and (5) truancy. If you engage in action such as non-attendance, or disruptive or defiant conduct (occupation of classrooms, blocking of doorways and hallways, etc.), you should realize that if school authorities so decide, they can suspend you or take other disciplinary action against you. *If this happens, you have no really effective legal defense available to you.*

Truancy

Any student who has been absent without valid excuse more than three days in one school year is reported as a truant. After this, two more absences without excuse can result in a declaration of habitual truancy. Habitual truants, or students who are "habitually insubordinate or disorderly during attendance at school," can be brought before the juvenile authorities. The juvenile authorities have the power to impose various sanctions, including sending you to the appropriate "opportunity school," or "continuation school."

Discipline and Procedure

If you are suspended, the school authorities must call in your parents for a conference. At that time, your parents can try to convince them not to punish you or to reduce the punishment. If you are expelled, you have a right to a hearing before the county board of education. In the event that you are suspended or otherwise disciplined, it might be helpful to contact an an attorney, or other competent person, to argue on your behalf at any conference or hearing that takes place. But any student who engages in activity such as that mentioned above (blocking doorways, disrupting classes, etc.) cannot rely on any "legal right" not to be punished.

Protected First Amendment Activity

High school students do have First Amendment rights. You cannot be totally prohibited from engaging in First Amendment activity. There is a potential conflict between your exercise of free speech rights and the right of school authorities to establish and enforce rules of conduct for students. In the recent Supreme Court case of *Tinker v. Des Moines School District*, 393 U.S. 503 (1969), a group of high school students were suspended for wearing black armbands in protest of the war in Vietnam. The United States Supreme Court held that the school authorities could not deny the rights of those students to express themselves in this manner.

The court, in its opinion, cited *Burnside v. Byars* for the proposition that student expression of opinion could not be prohibited unless such expression would "materially and substantially interfere with the requirements of appropriate discipline in the operation of the school." This means that if you carry out your political activity in such a way as not to interfere with the normal functioning of the school, it is constitutionally protected.

Leafletting

You can legally distribute written material so long as such distribution does not interfere with the normal functioning of the school (during non-class hours and in areas where school operations are not disrupted). The distribution of literature which uses obscene language, or which advocates unlawful acts, such as truancy, is probably not constitutionally protected.

Posting Notices

The posting of signs in areas normally used for that purpose appears to be constitutionally protected. If an area is reserved, however, for official school notices, the interest of the school authorities is sufficient to prohibit you from posting signs in that area. But in areas normally used for student notices, especially if political literature has been posted there in the past, the school personnel cannot forbid you to post signs merely because they do not like their content.

Political Gathering

The school has the constitutional right to prescribe regulations regarding the time, place and manner of rallies and assemblies. You should try to obtain permission in advance if you want to hold an assembly on school grounds. The school probably cannot totally prohibit *all* such gatherings. These and other activities cannot, however, be carried on in such a way as to substantially interfere with school operations. The constitution does not protect students who engage in activities such as non-attendance, disruption of classes, blocking of doorways, etc. Mere controversy and differences of opinion arising out of otherwise peaceful conduct, however, does not constitute the sort of disruption that will justify the prohibition of that activity.

School authorities may cite the California Education Code, section 9013, which prohibits the distribution of circulars or bulletins, the purpose of which is to "spread propaganda," on school premises during school hours or within one hour before or after school, and section 9021 which prohibits the solicitation of students to contribute to, become members of, or work for, any organization not under the control of school members except for certain non-partisan charitable organizations. They might tell you these statutes mean you cannot leaflet, etc. Explain to them that a federal court has recently restrained the Richmond School District from applying section 9013. By the time you read this, these statutes will probably have been declared unconstitutional.

Practical Considerations
     The fact that you have certain rights does not necessarily mean that those rights will be respected. It is possible that school authorities will try to stop you from exercising those few rights which you do have. The best procedure to follow, if you intend to engage in some sort of political activity on campus, is to talk with the principal of your school and get permission in advance. If he refuses, tell him about the *Tinker* case, and explain that you have a constitutional right to engage in non-disruptive political activity. If he continues to refuse permission, it might help to contact an attorney or someone with a knowledge of the law who can speak with the principal about the rights of students, or take whatever other action is needed.

     2. Private. Private high school students are in the same boat as private high school teachers. At present, you are virtually "rightless" and have only as much freedom to participate in political activity at school as your administration is willing to give you. See p. 55.

IV. Legislation on Campus Disruption

A. *Criminal Penalties*

     The law requires the chief administrative officer of every state institution of higher education (i.e., community college and state college presidents, and University of California chancellors) to take disciplinary action against any student or employee (academic or non-academic) who is convicted of any crime arising out of a campus disturbance or who is found by a campus investigating board to have willfully engaged in disruptive conduct, CAL EDUCATION CODE § 22505. The rules on campus disruption have been discussed in the sections on college students. There are several penal laws which may be violated during campus political protests. The penal code provides that it is a misdemeanor to disturb the peace of any state institution of higher education by loud noise, offensive conduct, threatening or challenging to fight, or profane language (§ 415.5); to obstruct or attempt to obstruct any student or teacher seeking to attend or instruct classes at any state institution of higher education by means of physical force or resistance (a person convicted under this section may be fined up to $500 or imprisoned for up to one year or both. There is no minimum penalty and no special provision for multiple convictions) (§ 602.10); threaten any officer or employee of an educational institution (public or private) with unlawful bodily harm or property damage in an attempt to influence him in the performance of his official duties (§ 71). The penalty for this last offense is up to five years in jail and/or a $500 fine.

In 1969 a number of provisions were passed allowing college and high school administrators to exclude certain people from campuses and providing criminal penalties for failure to leave. Under these laws, a non-member of the campus community of any state institution of higher education may be asked to leave the campus where it reasonably appears that he has committed or is likely to commit "any act likely to interfere with the peaceful conduct" of campus activities, CAL PENAL CODE § 626.6. Similarly, any person on or around any public or private high school ground without lawful business there may be asked to leave if his acts or presence interfere with the peaceful conduct of school activities, CAL PENAL CODE § 626.8. Notice that non-campus members can be excluded more easily from high school grounds. In both cases, failure to leave upon request or returning within seventy-two hours is a misdemeanor.

Further, the chief administrative officer (or his delegate) on a campus of a state institution of higher education may require that any person who is reasonably suspected of willfully disrupting the orderly operation of that campus absent himself from that campus for a period not to exceed two weeks. Entry upon such campus before such period expires, or before permission to enter the campus is restored, is a misdemeanor, CAL PENAL CODE § 626.4. Section 626.6 above and this section are quite similar but there are three significant differences between them. First, 626.6 applies only to non-members of the campus community, while 626.4 appears to apply to both members and non-members. Second, 626.6 requires a lesser showing (acts "likely to interfere with the peaceful conduct" of campus activities) and is effective for only seventy-two hours while 626.4 requires a more stringent showing (willful disruption) and may be effective up to two weeks. Third, if a person is banished from the campus under 626.4, he may, within the two week period, request a hearing and must be granted such a hearing within seven days of the time the administrative officer receives the request.

Finally, it is a misdemeanor for any dismissed or suspended student or employee of a state institution of higher education to knowingly enter upon such institution without written permission, where such student or employee was denied access to that institution as a condition of his dismissal or suspension, CAL PENAL CODE § 626.2. Multiple convictions for any of the § 626 misdemeanors will lead to mandatory increased punishment. The first conviction under any of the above statutes is punishable by up to six months in jail or a $500 fine or both, but with no minimum penalty imposed. In the case of a second conviction under the same statute, or a conviction under another of the above statutes, the defendant is subject to the same maximum penalties, but must serve a minimum of ten days in jail. For a third such conviction, the maximum punishment is still the same, but the defendant must serve a minimum of ninety days in jail.

B. *Use of Educational Institution's Name*

It is a misdemeanor for any person or group to invoke or use the name of the University of California in connection with political activities. No organization or group may use the words "University of California" (or any abbreviation thereof) in its name without the express permission of the University, CAL EDUCA-TION CODE § 23001. This law does not prevent any person or group from truthfully stating its relationship to the University. Thus a group could not lawfully call itself the University of California Antiwar Front; but a group called the Berkeley Antiwar Front or even the Berkeley Campus Antiwar Front could legally state that its membership is composed of students and faculty of the University of California (if that is in fact the case). Furthermore, one who is a student, a faculty member, or an employee of the University is always free to state that fact, provided he does not imply that he is speaking for the University.

State college students may not use the name of the California State Colleges, either, but to do so subjects them to college disciplinary proceedings rather than criminal penalties, 5 CAL. ADMINISTRATIVE CODE § 41301. Junior colleges and high schools are likely to have a similar rule.

C. *Injunctions and Temporary Restraining Orders*

In the judgment of the editor a technique for handling political protest activities on campuses that is likely to be used increasingly by authorities in the future is the injunction. Administrators have no real need to call police on campus to carry out sit-in protestors, or to drive off any other individuals who "disrupt" public buildings, if they can get (and they usually can) an immediate temporary restraining order from the court. When it later becomes a permanent injunction, such a restraining order may be used days or weeks later as a lever for punishing protestors. Thus administrators can avoid adding "fuel to the fire" by going in with police at the time of a protest. The officials can seek an injunction by filing a complaint, generally accompanied by sworn affidavits, alleging the existence of a repeated or continuous trespass (in the case of a sit-in, other misdemeanors can be alleged where appropriate) and, in general terms, the danger of irreparable harm and the lack of an adequate remedy at law. The complaint will end with a request for a permanent injunction against the trespass, and in the meantime a temporary restraining order may and quite possibly will be granted without representation of the parties and without notice of the proceeding. This technique has been used at Columbia University and at the University of California at San Diego. These temporary restraining orders are "only intended to restore and preserve the last peaceful status quo of the parties," i.e., to get the protestors out of the building, off campus or whatever. In the judgment of the editor, this can amount to a trial and conviction without benefit of notice, hearing or jury. Should the protestor fail to "restore" the previous status, i.e., leave the building, he will be in contempt and eligible for fine and/or imprisonment. He will also be subject to prosecution for the substantive crime of trespass. Understandably this technique can be misused. There are good grounds for believing that particular applications may be a violation of the Due Process clause of the XIV Amendment and other Constitutional rights. This is a matter which should be discussed with legal counsel if you or your group are confronted with such a situation. The most informative article on the question of the use of injunctions, as well as an excellent, highly readable companion article on legislative reactions to campus unrest, may be found in the *Columbia University Journal of Law and Social Problems,* Vol. 6, No. 1 (January, 1970), p. 1.

D. *Revocation of Student Financial Aid*

Students involved in activities which disrupt University operations risk the loss of certain types of state and federal financial aid.

1. Federally-aided Programs. Since 1968 Congress has enacted a number of restrictions on the distribution of federal funds as aid to students involved in disruptive activities. Most of these restrictions resemble section 504(a) and (b) of Public Law 90-575 (1968). This section provides that when an educational institution determines that a student either (a) has been convicted of a crime involving the use of force, disruption, or seizure of property to prevent officials or students from engaging in their duties or pursuing their studies and that such crime was "of a serious nature" and "contributed to a substantial disruption of the institution," or (b) has willfully violated a valid school regulation or order and that the violation was serious and disruptive of the institution's administration, the institution shall deny any further financial aid to the student for a period of two years.

This section may be invoked only after the students affected have had notice and an opportunity for a hearing. The financial aids which may be terminated under this provision include Educational Opportunity grants, federally insured student loans, the work-study program, and National Defense Education Act loans and fellowships. Other restrictions apply to a number of other types of federally financed aid, including grants and loans for health education, Cuban student loans, student loans arranged through states and nonprofit organizations, R.O.T.C. funds, and N.S.F. fellowships. The circumstances which can invoke these restrictions include the criminal convictions and regulation violations listed above and also conviction of "inciting, promoting, or carrying on a riot, or other [illegal] group activity resulting in material damage to property or injury to persons." Some of these provisions require that aid be withheld immediately following criminal conviction, without regard to notice or hearing. Since Congress in the last two years has enacted provisions of this sort at least nine times, it is possible that every kind of federal student aid may soon be covered. On the other hand, many of the restrictions are contained in appropriations bills and will remain in force only for the duration of the appropriations. If the restrictions are not re-enacted they will become inoperative within a few years. (See, for example, the following Public Laws: 90-132, 90-373, 90-550, 90-557, 90-575, 90-580, 91-120, 90-126, and 91-204.)

Since the fall of 1969 it has been University of California policy to invoke restrictions of this type when they are applicable, and some procedures have been formulated for that purpose. Under present plans the decision to end financial aid would be made separately from the ordinary disciplinary procedures. No Berkeley students have yet been affected but aid has been terminated under these restrictions at other universities. The activity most likely to result in such terminations would seem to be seizure of university buildings. It should be noted that several of the federal laws listed above do not preclude universities from denying aid to recipients whose conduct the university believes "bears adversely on their fitness" to receive support even though that conduct is not the type covered in the federal restrictions. Whether schools have independent power to deny aid on these vague grounds depends upon the terms of the particular aid in question. It seems unlikely, however, that such power will be invoked at the University of California, except, perhaps, to end unusual types of aid. Students at state and junior college campuses should try to determine the policies of their schools on terminating federal aid.

2. State Financial Aids. The California legislature has also enacted restrictions on the distribution of financial aid to students involved in disruptive acts at an institution of higher learning. The new sections 31292 to 31294 of the Cal. Education Code allow state aid to be withheld for up to two years from any recipient found by court conviction or school hearing to have willfully disrupted the educational institution. Further, any student who is suspended by his school for taking part in such a disruption is ineligible for state aid for the period of his suspension. Like the federal provisions, these Education Code sections preserve whatever power colleges and universities formerly possessed to suspend aid when they feel a recipient's conduct "bears adversely on his fitness" to receive it. Although these sections could be interpreted as applying to all types of aid coming directly or indirectly from the state (such as Regents scholarships and loans and University loans and prizes), it appears that the section will cover only California State Scholarships.

3. Other Ways in Which Aid May Be Affected. Finally, there are several indirect ways in which a student's financial support may be jeopardized by participation in campus disturbances. First, some aid programs are by their terms contingent upon the student's continued satisfactory class performance or his full-time student status. These programs, such as work-study, may be interrupted or canceled when a student is suspended through disciplinary action or when he drops or fails his courses. Under the Regents' Resolutions issued March 20, 1970, whenever a state of emergency is declared on campus, interim suspension shall be imposed on any student, faculty member, or employee when there is reasonable cause to believe he has violated campus regulations by disruptive acts. Further, if a hearing discloses that the individual did violate such regulations, he is subject to a minimum of suspension for one quarter.

Second, students with university jobs may find them jeopardized by participation in disturbances. Suspension under the Regents' Resolutions applies to both students and employees, and the Penal Code provision restricting campus access seems to preclude at least temporarily the performance of university jobs. Interim suspension is a flexible procedure which may or may not prevent a student from working on campus. Finally, the regular employee disciplinary procedure (with provision for employee grievances) can be applied to student employees although the student disciplinary procedure usually supersedes it. When any of these procedures are applied, student employees wil lose their pay for the period during which they cannot work, and may in addition lose their jobs.

4. Constitutional Issues. Questions have been raised as to the constitutionality of these restrictions on financial aid. The provisions may be vague and over-

broad, and deficiencies in the hearing procedure may constitute a denial of due process. Finally, the restrictions may be discriminatory in affecting only those who must rely on financial aid. In view of the uncertainty of the law and the time and expense involved in testing them, reliance on these constitutional issues is not recommended.

V. Non-Students on Campus

A. *University of California*

While on campus you are subject to University and campus rules and the same conduct rules that students are, UNIVERSITY POLICIES, p. 10. To find out what these are, consult the section on U.C. students, p. 58.

There are certain restrictions on your activities. You may not use the campus for fund raising unless you represent a charitable organization or public service agency and then only with the permission of the Chancellor. You may not address campus meetings unless you are invited by the University, a registered student organization, a University employee organization, an official University alumni association, or a member of the teaching or administrative staff. Non-university organizations may use University facilities only with the prior approval of the Chancellor and "for purposes which are not incompatible with the functions of the University." Finally, you are not permitted, unless the Chancellor so specifies, to "post, distribute free of charge, and exhibit noncommercial materials." This somewhat ambiguous provision could be interpreted to exclude the passing out of political leaflets on campus, but if it is so interpreted, it is almost certainly unconstitutional, *Mandel v. Superior Court,* 276 A.C.A. 788 (1969), discussed in IV. below.

As a practical matter, the University campuses are generally open to the public, and public participation in on-campus free expression activities is a daily occurrence. Nonetheless, you should be aware that while on campus, you are legally obligated to obey all University and campus rules, identify yourself if asked to do so by a University official, and leave the campus if so directed, UNIVERSITY POLICIES, p. 10.

B. *State Colleges.* The state-wide rules adopted by the Trustees for the conduct of political activities on campus make no distinction between members and non-members of the campus community. See the section on State College students for a discussion of these rules. See section IV above for laws governing your to enter and remain on the campus grounds.

C. *Community or Junior Colleges.* The Education Code is singularly silent on the rights and obligations of the public on junior college campuses. Individual junior college districts may, however, have regulations governing the public on campus. You can obtain such information from the administrative office.

If such rules are not available, several general principles govern your conduct. First, the *Mandel* case would apply to junior colleges as well as high schools (see section on high schools, part D below), which means that you at least have a right to pass out unobscene, unsubversive leaflets in a way that does not interfere with the normal functions of the school. The college probably can require you to get permission to solicit money and use college facilities.

Finally, a state-wide code of conduct for junior college students, due to come out in the fall of 1970, may contain regulations which apply to the public on campus.

D. *Secondary Schools.* Certain areas of all schools are designated "civic centers" and may be used by any group for educational or political activities, so long as this use does not interfere with school activities, EDU-CATION CODE § 16556. Thus, school district officials may not prohibit any group from holding a meeting of any kind inside the school after school hours. They may require permits and a "reasonable" waiting period between the date of application and the date granted for the meeting, but if there are no other groups competing for the use of the building, or if there are other buildings available, anything longer than seventy-two hours is probably unreasonable.

Moreover, non-students may pass out literature on school property as long as such activity does not disrupt school functions, *Mandel v. Superior Court,* 276 A.C.A. 788 (1969). *Mandel* stated that: " 'In order for . . . school officials to justify prohibition (on school premises) of a particular expression of opinion (they) must be able to show that (their) action was caused by something more than a mere desire to avoid the discomfort and unpleasantness that always accompany an unpopular viewpoint.' "

VI. Aliens

A. *Foreign Students*

Foreign students may participate in political activities (including leafletting, petitioning, marching, etc.) without fear of repercussion from the Immigration and Naturalization Service as long as they do not (1) lose their student status, (2) advocate or get involved in illegal or violent activities, or (3) advocate or involve themselves in subversive activities. In short, they may participate in protected speech activities to virtually the same extent as American students.

Foreign students (F and J visa holders) who pursue a full course of study in an established institution of learning will not lose their status unless they fall within one of the "deplorable alien" categories listed in 8 U.S.C. § 1251. Those categories dealing with political activity provide for deportation of aliens whom Congress has deemed dangerous to the national security, i.e., persons who preach and practice forcible overthrow of the American form of government, advocate world communism or who have a knowing and "meaningful" association with the Communist Party and its auxiliaries. Also deportable are aliens who engage in activities prohibited by laws on espionage, sabotage or maintenance of public order, or who are subversive to the national security or "prejudicial to the public interest or endanger the welfare, safety or security of the United States," 8 U.S.C. § 1182 (a)(27).

While the district director of the immigration office has considerable discretion concerning granting, extension and revocation of visa status, he cannot legally deport foreign students for reasons other than those stated in § 1251. He is not likely to pay much attention to traditional political activities, although foreign students who become prominent leaders in the more activist, radical activities may be called in for an interview.

Foreign students who are arrested will not necessarily be deported. Minor offenses are generally passed over, although, of course, convictions of more serious offenses are not. Foreign students should check with their *own* consulate if they have any doubts about their country's approval of their political activities. Actions which may not get them in trouble with American authorities could get them in trouble with their own.

B. *Other Non-Immigrants*

In general, all other persons holding non-immigrant visas may engage in the same activities as those described for foreign students above. As with students, there is the possibility that they may lose their status if they cease doing the activity which is the stated basis for their visa (e.g., business, temporary work). However, they are less likely to come to the attention of the Immigration and Naturalization Service if there is not an organization (like a university) continually supervising their status.

VII. Tax Exempt Organizations

The tax statutes and regulations do not totally prohibit tax exempt organizations from engaging in political activities. However, they do impose several restrictions that circumscribe the character and amount of such activities.

A. *The Statute.* 26 U.S.C. § 501(c)(3)

This section provides exemptions for:

"Corporations, and any community chest, fund, or foundation, organized and operated exclusively for religious, charitable, scientific, testing for public safety, literary, or educational purposes, or for the prevention of cruelty to animals or children, no part of the net earnings of which inures to the benefit of any private shareholder or individual, *no substantial part of the activities of which is carrying on propaganda, or otherwise attempting, to influence legislation, and which does not participate in, or intervene in (including the publishing or distributing of statements), any political campaign on behalf of any candidate for public office.*"

The underlined language is the key to the political rights of such organizations.

B. *The Regulations.* 26 C.F.R. § 1.501(c)(3)-1

The income tax regulations prescribe two tests: (a) organizational and (b) operational. The relevant provisions are as follows:

1. Organizational Test. The articles of organization may *not* "expressly empower the organization to engage, *otherwise than as an insubstantial part of its activities,* in activities which in themselves are not in furtherance of one or more exempt purposes." The thrust of this section is that the articles of exempt organizations *may not* empower them to:

(a) devote "more than an insubstantial part" of their activity to influencing legislation by propaganda or otherwise;

(b) participate directly or indirectly (including the publication and distribution of statements) in any political campaign for or against any candidate for public office;

(c) have objectives or activities which make it an "action organization."

2. Operational Test. Generally, an organization is an action organization if it attempts to influence legislation as a substantial part of its activities or if it participates in political campaigns. However, the regulations explicitly provide that:

"An organization will not fail to meet the operation test merely because it advocates, as an *insubstantial part of its activities,* the adoption or rejection of legislation."

Further, the regulations do not preclude "engaging in nonpartisan analysis, study or research and making the results available to the public." In the absence of any informative case law on the definition of "substantial" and "insubstantial," the following conclusions may be drawn with reasonable confidence:

(a) Exempt organizations *may* take positions and issue public statements on political issues.

(b) Exempt organizations *may* attempt to influence legislation (including through contributions), but this activity *may not* constitute more than an insubstantial part of their activities.

(c) Exempt organizations *may not* participate in political campaigns for or against any candidate.

In short, a statement opposing the war is part of advocating legislation to stop it, which activity is clearly permissible (so long as such activity is an insubstantial part of an organization's activities). Obviously, organizations that do not care about losing their tax exempt status can be very vocal. However, most organizations must carefully appraise their present levels of political activity (e.g., lobbying for legislation). If they do not engage in any political activities at all, they may certainly issue a statement calling for antiwar legislation without fear of reprisals. If they already push the limits of "insubstantiality" (approximately 5%), they must proceed with caution.

Note: The statute and regulations *do not* preclude the issuance of statements condemning *executive* action. Thus, for example, statements may condemn the executive for waging an undeclared war and call upon congress to reassert its constitutional perogatives.

VIII. Military Personnel

The rights of military personnel to engage in anti-war activities are extremely limited. The Law: The Uniform Code of Military Justice (UCMJ-10 U.S.C. § 801 *et seq.*) applies to members of a regular component of the armed forces, cadets and midshipmen, certain members of reserve components, and military prisoners, among others. It lists a series of offenses that may trigger court martial proceedings (§§ 877-934). The list includes several that are relevant to political activities: conspiracy (§ 881), riot or breach of peace (§ 916), provoking speeches or gestures (§ 917), conduct unbecoming an officer and a gentleman (officers) (§ 933), and, most important, General Article (§ 934):

Though not specifically mentioned in this Chapter, all disorders and neglects to the prejudice of good order and discipline in the armed forces, all conduct of a nature to bring discredit upon the armed forces . . . shall be taken cognizance of by a general, special or summary court-martial.

Interpretation: The General Article may be unconstitutional for vagueness and overbreadth. As yet, no court has said so. And, although judges often pay lip-service to the principle that soldiers do not forfeit their constitutional rights, the cases do not reveal an unswerving devotion to this principle in fact. In short, military personnel should be aware that you *risk* court-martial for almost any anti-war or other "anti-establishment" political activity.

IF YOU WANT TO DO SOMETHING: contact the nearest draft counseling service and they should be able to advise you as to your rights, or to put you in contact with someone who can do so.

CHAPTER THREE

IF YOU ARE ARRESTED

Being arrested is a serious matter. Even if you are never convicted the record of the arrest will remain to haunt you. Conviction is even worse, especially for a felony (almost any relatively serious crime). Thus, unless you want to get arrested (to further a political goal) the cardinal rule is *DO NOT GET ARRESTED*. If you are arrested, however, either intentionally or unintentionally, the hints in this chapter may help you get out of jail and avoid conviction.

I. Avoiding Arrest

There may be good reasons for committing civil disobedience and getting arrested, but unless you are convinced they apply to you at a particular time and place, you should try to avoid arrest even if it means sacrificing, for the time being, the activities you are engaged in—leafleting, picketing, etc. Although there are legal standards which in theory govern when the police can arrest you, as a practical matter it is useless to assert a right not to be arrested on the street. The first rule, therefore, is to *obey any order given you by the police*. Do not talk back.

In California a police officer can ask you to identify yourself and account for your presence. If you refuse, this is *in itself* a crime, CAL. PENAL CODE § 647. While there is reason to doubt the validity of this law, and it may not in its own terms even apply to you (you must be loitering or wandering without apparent purpose), unless you want to test the law in court you should comply. Give your name and address; tell the officer that you are going home, shopping, etc. unless it is obvious that you are doing something like leafleting. Don't give a lengthy explanation of your right to be where you are; this will only invite trouble.

The police may "frisk" you. They have the authority to pat down your outer clothing for weapons. Do not resist. Do not carry drugs or weapons of any kind, including a pen knife—and certainly not a rock.

If the person who approaches you is not in uniform, ask him—politely—for his identification. If it is obvious to you that he *is* a police officer, it's probably best to forego asking for identification—it may just antagonize him.

Above all, remain cool. Keep your anger and frustration inside. There are ways of getting protection against arrest when you go out to leaflet, etc., again.

II. If You Are Arrested

If an officer is determined to arrest you, he will. He need not say, "You're under arrest"—"Let's go" will do it. Trying to argue will only make it worse. Worst of all is physical resistance. You may well be injured, and will give the police a chance to charge you with one or more felonies. In California *any* form of resistance, even verbal or passive (like going limp), can be charged against you. Even if you think the arrest is illegal (even if it *is* illegal), you should not resist. It is a crime in

California to resist even illegal arrests. So *DO NOT RESIST ARREST*.

There are several things you can do to help yourself, and some other things you should not do:

(1) If you are going to a place where arrests may be expected—like a rally or demonstration—take plenty of cigarettes if you smoke; the Pill if you're on it. *DO* go with several people who know you. If they avoid arrest they will be able to get legal help to you, and later, to serve as witnesses.

(2) If you are in a crowd, *DO* yell out your name so that people can get help to you and be witnesses.

(3) *DO* try to get the badge number and department of the officer or officers who arrest you. If you are a witness, get this information and write it down with the name of the person arrested, and enough about the incident to enable you to testify later. Contact your local legal services office.

(4) *DO NOT* talk to the police. Before they question you they are supposed to warn you that

—you have a right to remain silent,

—anything you say can be used against you,

—you have a right to have a lawyer present when you are questioned, and

—if you can't afford a lawyer, one will be provided for you.

Even if they do not warn you or even question you, remember these rights. Tell them *ONLY* your name and address. *DO NOT* try to find out the charges against you.

(5) You have a right to make two completed telephone calls: to a relative or a lawyer, and to a bail bondsman, CAL. PENAL CODE § 851.5. *DO* carry enough money to make two calls. *DO* call a lawyer. If you don't know one, you can get legal help from your local Legal Switchboard or legal assistance office or from the American Civil Liberties Union. Before you go

out, write the number of at least one of these services on your arm; your wallet may be taken when you are booked. At least try to remember the name of one of these groups in your area. They should be able to get a lawyer to you the same day. Be prepared to tell the lawyer everything you can about the events surrounding your arrest.

III. Getting Out

A. *Adults*

You have a right to be released on bail, CAL PENAL CODE § 1271. It is also possible, but less likely, that you will be released by the arresting officer if you are charged with a misdemeanor, CAL PENAL CODE § 849(b)(3), or released on your "own recognizance," CAL PENAL CODE § § 1318-20. If you are charged with a misdemeanor, there is a bail schedule set for the offense charged. Theoretically, the clerk of the court must always be available to accept bail and release you, CAL PENAL CODE § 1269(b); CAL GOVERNMENT CODE § 72301. However, a judge may set a higher bail than the schedule provides. If you are charged with a felony, a judge will set the bail. The police are supposed to bring you before a judge "without unnecessary delay," CAL PENAL CODE § 849(a).

Any of the legal services offices can help you to raise bail or get bail reduced (especially in the case of a felony). A bail bondsman will sell you your freedom for 10 percent of the amount of the bail. If there is a bail project in your area, they can try to get you released on your own recognizance, i.e., without payment of money bail.

If you come before a judge, do NOT enter a plea to the charges (not even "not guilty"). Ask for a continuance so that you can consult a lawyer.

B. *Juveniles*

A juvenile does *not* have a right to be released on bail. Rather, after he is arrested, he is "delivered" to a juvenile probation officer unless the arresting officer releases him. The probation officer must immediately release the juvenile, "unless it appears that further detention . . . is a matter of immediate and urgent necessity." (See CAL WELFARE AND INSTITUTIONS CODE, 625 *et seq.*) In other words, they can keep you under wraps. These provisions automatically apply to you if you are under 16; if between 16 and 21 they may apply. Juveniles DO have a right to a lawyer and to remain silent, however. Even if you are being treated as a juvenile call a lawyer. The probation officer is not your friend; he is basically a prosecutor. He will likely be more amenable to releasing you if you play the role but it is still not advisable to talk to him about the events leading to your arrest without a lawyer's advice. If you are not convicted, it may be possible to have the arrest record sealed so that your record appears as if you never had been arrested, CAL PENAL CODE 851.7.

References

For further information on avoiding arrest, how to act in a demonstration, and what to do if you are arrested, see K. Boudin *et al., The Bust Book,* Grove Press, 1970, $1.25 paperback. For further information on bail, see Comment, *Tinkering with the California Bail System,* 56 *California Law Review,* 1134, 1138-41, 1152-55 (1968).

INDEX

[94]

THE DEMOCRACY DEFENDED SERIES

The organizational expression of the political and moral perspective now embodied in the World Without War Council began in 1958. Committed since then to the radical goal of ending war, the Council has worked in many ways to develop alternatives to a dominately U.S. military foreign policy. Out of its commitment to non-violent conflict resolution and to democratic values, the Council has opposed the trends toward revolutionary politics on the campuses and in the peace movement.

The publication of the *Democracy Defended Series* is in a sense a new venture, but one consistent with our continuing commitment to democratic values and institutions. In the late 1950's, political discourse in this country was generally characterized by a complacent assessment of the viability of democratic institutions. Today attacks on democratic procedures and institutions are not only respectable, they dominate important segments of the community. In such a political climate too few students ever encounter, much less thoughtfully consider, the justifications for democracy and the capacity of democratic institutions for problem solving. Publications in this series will seek to meet the current attacks on democratic theory and practice with reasoned rebuttals.

The first part of the *Democracy Defended Series* reaffirms a belief in democratic values, procedures and institutions considered in the context of domestic U.S. politics. A second part of the series, the *Democracy Extended* publications, brings together a series of books and pamphlets which argue that democratic values should guide our relations with the third world and with the Communist nations and should shape our participation in international organizations. Since any defense of democratic theory and practice is likely to fail in the midst of a nuclear arms race if it does not find ways of resolving the problem of war, a third part of the series consists of *Modern Classics of Peace.* Together, the *Democracy Extended* and *Modern Classics of Peace* publications identify and develop the ideas essential to achieving a world without war.

The contemporary attack on democratic institutions and practices flows from many sources. Many unresolved problems and injustices provide fuel for such attacks. Thoughtful action to achieve needed change and redress injustice is one effective response to the current challenge to democratic institutions and practices. Americans are presently engaged in significant public and private attempts to improve the environment, to achieve better news media handling of controversial issues, to broaden public participation in political parties, to improve police /community relations, to redress discrimination against racial minorities, to find ways of prosecuting international conflict without war, and in establishing projects and changing laws to overcome poverty. The chances of resolving such problems are greatly increased when recognition of them is widespread, when reasonable debate about different ways to resolve them takes place and when policies are drafted and implemented which have majority support. It is just these functions which democratic procedures and institutions are designed to accomplish.

In a time when democratic politics are under attack by various right-wing minorities advocating racist or elitist government and by left-wing minorities advocating various forms of peoples' dictatorships, constructive work on other social and political problems needs to be combined with a defense of the procedures and institutions which make nonviolent resolution of such problems pos-possible. Our concern in this series is to examine those currents of anti-democratic thought which influence the student and peace movements and have become fashionable in some intellectual circles. Scholars, intellectuals and peace movement workers have in the past been among the staunchest defenders of democratic values, reasoned debate, and nonviolent political processes. It is a significant mark of the extremity of our current situation that today the challenge to democratic values and processes is raised not just in military, ultra-conservative and racist circles but also in the academic community and in the anti-war movement. In my view, it is the latter groups which can and should help to provide the moral ground and leadership for challenging and opposing anti-democratic tendencies growing in any segment of the society.

The initial publication in the series, *The Law and Political Protest,* identifies the activities open to individuals or organizations who wish to affect the public policy process in this country. The book describes the limits which may be placed upon the rights of political protest, limits set fundamentally by the need to protect the rights of others. Subsequent publications will address the following questions: Do modern technological societies co-opt all internal opposition movements by diverting their energies or buying them off? Is academic freedom a value and a practice which protects repressive social practices? Is American society ruled by a closed elite? On what values are democratic procedures and institutions based? Are there other forms of government more likely to defend and extend these values? Can civil disobedience be carried out in respect for law? How does civil disobedience differ from insurrectionary or revolutionary violence? Are democratic values and institutions relevant to the problems of modernizing societies? Does it make sense to consider ways and means of extending demo-

cratic institutions to military or authoritarian states? To
Communist states? Do democratic values provide guidelines for the conduct of international relations? For setting the goals of American foreign policy? Does the
human rights tradition, expressed in the U.S. Bill of
Rights and the U.N. Declaration of Human Rights, provide good standards for judging the performance of governments?

The *Democracy Defended Series* does not consider
these questions from all points of view. Attacks on democratic values and institutions have been widely dissem-
inated by the major publishers in this country and by a
variety of mass circulation newspapers and magazines.
The popular defenses of democracy frequently ignore the
problems which prompt the attacks. If New Left social
critics are right, we are faced with a dilemma. We must,
they say, choose between supporting an inert government
which is beholden to special interests and an exploitive
social structure, or join a violent opposition movement
which is, at least, committed to resolving our most immediate problems. The *Democracy Defended Series* will
speak to those who want to confront our society's domestic and international problems and are troubled by
current theoretical justifications for revolutionary violence. Before these justifications they stand uncertain and
out of that uncertainty and a commitment to needed
change frequently provide support for action which
undermines democratic belief and practice. Such individuals, for example, frequently confuse the need to defend
the civil liberties even of an anti-democratic opposition
with an unwarranted defense of acts which violate or
pose a clear and present danger to the civil liberties of
others.

One need not agree with current policies or adopt a
revolutionary posture to do meaningful work on our
social problems. But if one believes in resolving conflict
nonviolently, one does need to accept the desirability of

maintaining democratic institutions and processes as indispensible forums. The rights and procedures of our democratic traditions are not a hollow set of principles which exist only in a world of abstractions; they are powerful means for change which have in the past proved their capability for altering and even transforming social and economic conditions. The twentieth century is creating problems faster than any society has yet been able to solve them. Many of these problems arise from changes which also hold the promise of a better future for the majority of mankind. Americans are the first to face the difficulties of a largely affluent society with an advanced technology and a diversity of races and conceptions of social justice. While the gap between political ideals and practical realities is great in every existing political system, our society's success or failure in closing that gap bodes well or ill for the rest of mankind. The gravity of our problems and the appalling injustices of a world which daily shrinks as its population grows make even more critical the need to keep sight of our fundamental values. Government by consent is our best hope for closing the gap between our ideals and reality and our only hope for preserving those values.

The publications listed here are either available now or expected by January, 1971. Additional publications will be added later.

September, 1970   **Robert Woito**
          Series Editor

The Democracy Defended Series

1. **The Law and Political Protest: A Handbook to your Political Rights under the Law** by thirty second and third-year law students. A concise summary of the current application of general constitutional doctrines to

specific situations and an opportunity to consider current attacks on constitutional democracy. 112pp, 1970 $1.25

2. **On Pure Tolerance, A Critique of Criticism** by David Spitz. A leading advocate of freedom of speech replies to Herbert Marcuse, Barrington Moore, Jr., and Robert Wolff's **Critique of Pure Tolerance**. 16pp, $.50

3. **Notes on Future Politics** by Carl Stover. An intelligent discussion of democratic processes, their strengths and weaknesses, and how they can be improved. 14pp, $.50

4. **One Dimensional Pessimism, A Critique of Herbert Marcuse's Theories** by Allen Graubard. A careful critique of Marcuse's authoritarianism, his sense of despair and his method of social analysis. 13pp, $.50

5. **Civil Disobedience but not Insurrectionary Violence** by Robert Pickus, and **Revolution and Violence** by Mulford Sibley. The first essay disassociates genuine civil disobedience from insurrectionary violence and the second argues that revolutionary violence is counter-productive for those seeking an egalitarian society. 12pp, $.25

6. **The Obligation to Obey the Law** by Richard Wasserstrom. A carefully reasoned discussion of possible justifications for civil disobedience and the need to consider such justifications in the light of a primary obligation to obey the law. 24pp, $.50

Other books of interest to readers of this series are: **The Development of the Democratic Idea, Readings from Pericles to the Present,** Charles Sherover (ed.), $1.45; **Community Power,** by Nelson Polsby, $1.45; **The Power Structure, Political Process in American Society,** by Arnold Rose, $2.95; **Education and the Barricades,** by Charles Frankel, $1.50; **Anti-Politics in America** by John Bunzel, $1.95; **Patterns of Anti-Democratic Thought,** by David Spitz, $2.45; and **Obligation and the Body Politic,** by Joseph Tussman, $1.50.

THE DEMOCRACY DEFENDED SERIES

The Democracy Extended Series

7. **Democracy and Development**, Mike Cavanaugh, (ed.) Features a remarkably clear exchange between Robert Heilbroner and Dennis Wrong on the relevance of democratic institutions to development, plus background information and resources on ways to tip the balance toward rapid modernization in political freedom. 100pp, 1971, $.95.

8. **The Challenge of Democracy**, by John Strachey. A contrast between Communism and Western Democracy, their accomplishments and weaknesses and the prospects for world democracy. 46pp, $.60

9. **Vietnam Peace Proposals**, Robert Woito (ed.) An Anthology which sets criteria for judging alternative peace plans including consideration of how well they are likely to achieve the right of self-determination for the South Vietnamese people. 54pp, $.75

10. **American Power in the Twentieth Century**, by Michael Harrington. Outlines a democratic, internationalist role for the U.S. in its relationships with other nations. 52pp, $.50

11. **Support Czechoslovakia**, April Carter et al. A description of nonviolent demonstrations in Moscow, Sofia, Budapest and Warsaw against the Soviet Union's denial of the right of self-determination to Czechoslovakia. 64pp, $1.00

12. **To End War**, by Robert Pickus and Robert Woito. A full scale presentation—set in the context of a commitment to democratic values—of the ideas, books and or-organizations likely to help end war. 262pp, $1.95

Other books of interest to readers of this series are: **The Democratic Experience, Past and Prospects**, by Reinhold Niebuhr and Paul Sigmund, $2.25; **Overcoming**

World Hunger, Clifford Hardin (ed.) $2.25; **The Future of the Underdeveloped Countries, Political Implications of Economic Development,** by Eugene Staley, $2.95; **The Global Partnership, International Agencies and Economic Development,** Richard Gardner and Max Millikan (eds.), $2.95

Modern Classics of Peace Series

13. **The Universal Declaration of Human Rights,** United Nations publication. Sets standards for judging the performance of political systems. $.02.

14. **Neither Victims Nor Executioners** by Albert Camus. Camus calls for a rejection of violence as the first step toward building a community of mankind. Includes an introduction by Robert Pickus relating these ideas to the present state of the American Peace Movement. 28pp, $.25

15. **Introduction to World Peace through World Law,** by Grenville Clark and Louis Sohn. An indispensable and authoritative description of the need for world law which outlines two roads to achieving it. 54pp, $.50

16. **All Men Are Brothers,** by M. K. Gandhi. Selected by UNESCO, this anthology of Gandhi's writings reveal his keen insight into the strength of nonviolent coercion as an expression of love and as an instrument of justice. 253pp, $1.95

Other books of interest to readers of this series are: **The Arms Race,** by Philip Noel-Baker, $3.00; **The Family of Man,** a photographic essay, $2.25; **Charter of the United Nations and Statute of the International Court of Justice,** $.50; **Speak Truth to Power,** American Friends Service Committee, $.35; **Progress, Coexistence and Freedom** by Andrei Sakharov, $1.50; **Christian Pacifism in History** by Geoffrey Nuttal, $1.25; **Pacem in Terris,** Pope

THE DEMOCRACY DEFENDED SERIES

John XXIII, $.35; **A Study of War**, by Quincy Wright, $2.95.

The numbered items in the series (# 1-16) may be ordered individually or at bulk rates. The trade discount applies to bookstore orders, a 10% library discount is available. The other "books of related interest" selections may be ordered individually with no bulk or other discounts.

Order from: World Without War Council
1730 Grove Street
Berkeley, California 94709

AN AFTERWORD

The Law and Political Protest serves two important purposes. It answers questions political activists ask about their rights within our political system. Since that system is under attack this book also provides an occasion for such activists to consider whether they want to defend it.

The University of California Boalt Hall law students, responsible for the careful legal research involved, set out to provide an accurate summary of the rights of political protest within the American legal system. In accomplishing this task, they have prepared a most useful handbook, anticipating most questions regarding the specific application of constitutionally protected rights to many forms of political activity. As the authors indicate, the book is neither a substitute for professional legal advice nor a fully adequate guide to the law. The law does change. It is subject to different interpretations and may be administered differently in different jurisdictions. Despite these inherent limitations, the book is a valuable resource: it spells out, for those challenging policies with which they profoundly disagree, the breadth of their right to do so and the limits American law places on such rights.

The most cursory examination of this handbook reveals a political system that carefully legitimizes and protects opposition to governmental policy. Such a political system is rarely encountered in history. It is rare today. More common are political systems which offer incarceration in mental institutions or prisons, if not worse, to those whose challenge to the government consists of a handbill. Whatever one may feel about current action by

American legal authorities against those who organize for violence outside the law, such "repression" is different in kind from General Pyotr Grigorenko's sentence to a mental institution for having spoken against the invasion of Czechoslovakia, or Valerien Novodvorskya's incarceration for distributing a poem charging that there was a lack of freedom in the Soviet Union. Similar examples and worse abound today; to name just a few countries, in Greece, Czechoslovakia, Cuba, Brazil, North and South Vietnam, South Africa, or, for a particularly brutal instance, Chinese rule in Tibet.

In such a time, *The Law and Political Protest* serves a second important purpose. It provides an occasion for reflection on the beliefs and the action essential to defend and extend democratic institutions. Those that read it thoughtfully will have an opportunity to clarify their attitude toward contemporary currents of thought and action which can destroy such institutions. This afterword is addressed to all who would take advantage of that opportunity.

Most readers of this book are, I presume, fully alert to the dangers of governmental repression and prepared to make clear their opposition to governmental acts which threaten political freedom. Is there an equivalent understanding of the importance of resisting the attack on democratic values and processes when they are advanced by political forces labelled "black," "student" or "peace"?

Clearly there is not. The current correlation between a recognition of the need for change and a willingness to abandon responsibility to a nonviolent democratic political process provides the occasion for this Afterword. Too frequently one encounters just such a juxtaposition of attitudes.

Justifications for extra-legal violence as the necessary instrument of a humane politics are widely accepted today. They are in fact the fashion. Those committed to a politics of violence are touted not only in influential literary and political journals but in widely distributed Hollywood movies. Certain features of contemporary culture: hostility to reason, to the study of history, to careful thought, provide a protective surround. So specious arguments spread and systematically erode a sense of obligation to sustain one of history's nearest approximations to an open and democratic society.

The World Without War Council is committed to democratic values. We need political liberty to do our work. We seek alternatives to violence in political conflict and we believe law and democratic politics are one important form of nonviolent conflict resolution.

We therefore resist the attack on a nonviolent democratic process, especially when that attack, claiming to spring from opposition to war, distorts the values and the goals of the peace movement. For it is not simply the prevalence of these patterns of anti-democratic thought that is so dangerous today. It is their location. Contempt for majority rule, mob action to prevent others' right to speak or to teach, the murder of innocents, the disruption of trials, are today justified by a dangerously broad segment of the political left. The attitudes essential to sustain a democratic society are eroding in just those centers of energy and idealsm so crucial to hopeful change. Arguments fashioned to challenge the legitimacy of tyrannical regimes are misapplied to justify contempt for the procedures by which majority opinion is formed and justice under the law is dispensed in a democratic polity.

Is this a democratic polity? Does the clear gap between the democratic ideal and the realities of American politics and law reveal only a more complicated tyranny? Most readers will have encountered the argument that we possess the form but not the substance of a functioning democracy. When used to identify inequities and to move us to correct power imbalances that argument helps preserve and extend democratic processes. But what of its use to destroy these procedures—and the values and institutions that sustain them? What should be our attitude toward new elites attempting to impose their conception of justice by violence? What should be our response when such political groups, with no concept of accountability, assert that they speak for "the people" and thus are beyond the authority of the law?

The rocks and bombings, the fires and bullets of those that would impose their will on the community, are not the central problem for those committed to democratic values and processes. Those engaged in revolutionary violence can burn and kill. They can damage a democratic society. They cannot alone destroy it.

It is the *response* to such attacks on an open and nonviolent public policy process that is crucial. Indiscriminate governmental repression is one disastrous response. An impotent or demoralized silence or worse, statements of support by those ostensibly opposed to such methods, is another road to the disintegration of a democratic polity. Too many committed to needed change are now on that road.

A single phrase, "I don't believe in violence, but . . ." takes us to the heart of the matter. For too often what follows the "but" is a series of justifications for the abandonment of responsibility to democratic values and to a nonviolent political process.

As Professor Sanford Kadish has observed in his statement, "More on Rock Throwing," there is the argument that "the ends sought—the elimination of ROTC and other University involvements with the military, for example—justify arson, vandalism and rock throwing. To me, this is practical and moral folly.

"It is practical folly because a progressively minded minority will not prevail by fire and rocks. By these tactics they invite new evils rather than effectively combat old ones. Converts to peace and justice are not won by such means, which rather alienate and embitter the great majority of citizens and prepare them to support measures of repression far worse than anything we have yet witnessed in this country. Fire and rocks can surely destroy the life of a University—but only as a prelude to the destruction of other humane and civilized features of our society, not to their growth and proliferation.

"It is moral folly because the ends sought—the ends of peace and social justice—are fatally corrupted by resort to private violence and terror as the means. These ends call for stopping the burning and destruction in the world. These means extend such acts to new communities. The tactics of violence are generally defended by those who use them as necessary to achieve greater ends. This is the historic justification for wars and violence, certainly including our participation in the war in Vietnam. We lose our moral ground entirely when our conduct, in character even if not in degree, becomes indistinguishable from that of our moral adversaries."

It is argued that the horror of governmental violence pales into insignificance individual acts of violence, even the death of an innocent man in the bombing of a public building. One can understand the force of this argument reading of the My Lai killings or, to consider the violence of other governments, the systematic and secret executions North Vietnamese forces conducted in Hue. One can understand yet firmly reject the confusions of this argument. For if one accepts this argument, what acts are to be denied those who take the horrors of war—or the acts of a totalitarian government—as standards for *their* conduct in pursuing political ends? With such standards, what action follows? The fact of monumental evils elsewhere does not reduce the moral responsibility of those engaged in present evil here. Nor does it lessen the responsibility of those committed to challenging governmental violence to resist private acts of terror and violence.

Another form of this argument excuses a violent minority's abuse of other's rights by equating such force with the coercion, sometimes violent, of the police. A monopoly on the legitimate use of violence is one defining characteristic of government. That such violence is used disproportionately and inappropriately at times no one should doubt. But to use this fact to legitimize the private use of violence for political ends in a democratic society is surely mistaken. The police are organized to operate within carefully prescribed rules, which the community establishes through its representatives. There is provision for restricting and punishing those law enforcement officers who violate these rules and misuse the trust placed in them by the community. Even those that doubt this description should ask whether political groups seeking to impose their minority will by violence and operating under *no* such restraints represent an advance. Do they prefer self-appointed elites using violence without the community's sanction—or for that matter without any sanction other than their own fallible vision?

Although government by consent does not always prevent abuse of power, deprivation of rights and other inequities, it does, better than any other political system, maximize the changes that such inequities will be discovered and corrected. Opposition to police excesses can be used to justify private violence and terror only if one no longer values a democratic political system.

Do we? That is, after all, the central question. Do we still understand and appreciate the practical wisdom of our democracy? Not simply its principled ground: government by consent, the idea that the people shall rule, the gradually developing concept of a government of laws that protects us from the arbitrary use of power and insists that the state is the servant and not the master of man; but its practical wisdom.

The problems we face are old ones: war, poverty, exploitation. The solutions are not obvious. Free speech is more than an individual right. It is an essential requisite for wise governmental policy. So is a rational, and open and nonviolent political process. Such a political process is now threatened by the acts of private groups as well as by state authorities. We know how to resist governmental incursions. Will we also resist a self-chosen elite which rejects the procedures by which a majority is formed and seeks to impose its minority will by violence? If we do not resist, will we be any closer to an end to war or to social justice?

I do not argue that preservation of the mechanisms of a nonviolent democratic system is the *primary* value and that any horror must run its course if supported by the majority. I do argue that these mechanisms give us our best chance of arriving at policies capable of resolving our problems. They are worthy of defense just because they do provide for the nonviolent resolution of conflicts that inevitably arise between competing policies, goals and interest, and because they offer nonviolent methods for correcting the distribution of power that would distort such a resolution.

In a time when awareness of the need for change is widespread, and the appeals of a politics of violence are carried to every home, we would do well to consider anew the value of a nonviolent democratic political system.

Another confusion in the present discussion is the ease with which insurrectionary violence and acts which set a favorable climate for such violence take on the moral mantle of nonviolent civil disobedience. Father Daniel Berrigan, who hid from Federal authorities to avoid imprisonment for an attack on a local draft board office, lays claim to the tradition of Socrates, Thoreau, and Gandhi, even as he violates that tradition's central premises. Socrates did not place himself above the law or outside its jurisdiction even when he openly refused to comply. Nor did Thoreau. Gandhi did not destroy other's offices to make his resistance effective. It takes an extra-ordinarily troubled political climate, one of surpassing unreason for insurrectionary values and actions to masquerade as civil disobedience even as such action seeks to evade, not accept, the law's penalty.

The withdrawal of consent in acts of genuine civil disobedience can help build the anti-war movement and can strengthen democratic institutions. It is another matter when such action is set in an alienated context and conducted as an act of disassociation from, not commitment to, our society. Action which does not reject violence, which teaches not respect for law but the most extreme hostility to it and to those responsible for its enforcement, has little to do with civil disobedience and is no aid in closing the gap between our commitment to a democratic society and undemocratic practices. It will not build a successful anti-war movement. When Daniel Berrigan, a humane and sensitive man, blurs these differences he contributes to a climate of violence which threatens our democracy and a genuine anti-war movement.

The aspirations of many now committed to dissent, their willingness to undertake great tasks and undergo personal hardship to achieve their goals is one of the most encouraging elements in contemporary politics. There is most hope for such aspirations when our moral ground is clearly distinguished from that of would-be or actual executioners, when the pursuit of great ends is joined to a commitment to a political system capable without violence of producing the agreement essential to their achievement.

The legitimacy of minority dissent is as valuable and essential as the right of the majority to govern, for it is only through such dissent that new problems and old grievances can gain the spirited advocates needed for their recognition and resolution. But there are limits to a political minority's rights. When a private group begins stockpiling weapons, when it threatens violence or in other ways denies the rights of others, societal protection ends and governmental repression will surely begin. No one who lives in an area where a policeman is murdered simply because he is a policeman, in which a Black Panther leader praises as politically desirable the kidnap slaying of a judge; where the underground press regularly exhorts its readers to "off a pig" and idolizes leaders of political systems in which conceptions of individual rights are almost entirely absent; where conceptions of civil disobedience which, even in resistance to a particular law remain committed to our legal system, are replaced by acts which seek to dismantle that system; where the campus community remains deeply divided over whether to condemn such activity or blame it on the abuses of the "system"—no one living in such a political environment should underestimate the clarity of belief and action required to sustain a democratic system. Nor should he underestimate the need for such action.

I have not addressed here those that want power to impose their "revolutionary" values and are willing to kill to get it and keep it. Nor do I address those that find "freedom" in the governmental practices of Mainland China or North Korea. Their arguments require a different response. I address those that reject such Orwellian Newspeak. It is those vulnerable to the appeal to violence when that appeal is joined to the false promise that it will help end the killing in Vietnam or achieve racial justice, who are, in my view, the key to our present crisis. They will either pass on, unexamined, distorted and untrue attacks on "the system"; attacks which set the moral climate for violence or they will challenge such attacks. They will either identify those engaged in violence as political opponents to be resisted or they will say, "I don't believe in violence, but . . ."

Do not underestimate the importance of the choice. Some will continue to provide a protective surround for assaults on a democratic political process; others will clearly and explicitly resist such attacks while continuing to work for needed change. In such resistance as in their work for change they defend the political rights of us all. They keep open the possibility of realizing democracy's promise.

September, 1970   **Robert Pickus**
President,
World Without War Council

1. Robert Pickus and Robert Woito, **To End War, An Introduction to the Ideas, Books, Organizations that can help.** 261pp, 1970, paperback (hereafter pb.) $1.95 The best layman's introduction to twelve war/peace fields, 600 books, over 100 organizations and 50 periodicals. A concise yet comprehensive presentation of the case for considering ending war as a practical goal, one which should guide our consideration of war/peace issues.

2. Albert Camus, **Neither Victims Nor Executioners,** 28pp, 1968, pamphlet (hereafter pam.) $.25 Camus' classic essay opposing the use of violence to gain political objectives with an introduction by Robert Pickus relating Camus' themes to the current American peace movement.

3. Grenville Clark & Louis Sohn, **Introduction to World Peace through World Law.** 54pp, 1967, pam., $.50 A cogent summary of how the U.N. can be made a genuine instrument of world law.

4. Allan Blackman, **Face to Face with Your Draft Board: A Guide to Personal Appearances.** 103pp, 1970, pb., $.95 This book is designed for conscientious objectors and is valuable to all men facing a personal appearance before their draft board. It helps to clarify fundamental beliefs while assisting the reader in obtaining the classification he wants and deserves.

5. Arlo Tatum, **Handbook for Conscientious Objectors.** 110pp, 1970, pb., $1.00 Emphasizes the problems of conscientious objectors, broadly defined, and others confronting the draft.

6. Michael Harrington, **American Power in the Twentieth Century.** 52pp, 1968, pam., $.50 The author of **The Other America**, which started the war on poverty, outlines a democratic, internationalist approach to foreign policy.

7. Robert Woito (ed.), **Vietnam Peace Proposals.** 54pp, 1967, rev. with current NLF and Nixon Peace Proposals, 1970, pam., $.75 An anthology which sets criteria for judging the peace proposals of the U.S., N.L.F. and North Vietnam as well as proposals for escalation, withdrawal, and American peace initiatives.

8. George Rathjens, **The Future of the Strategic Arms Race: Options for the 1970's.** 65pp, 1969, pam., $.60 Clarifies many of the complex disarmament and arms control issues by examining the basic premises of deterrence.

9. M. K. Gandhi, **All Men Are Brothers**. 253pp, 1968, pb., $1.95 An anthology of Gandhi's writings, selected by UNESCO, including portions of his autobiography and selections on peace, democracy, poverty and nonviolence. English edition, printed in India.

10. April Carter et al., **Support Czechoslovakia**. 64pp, 1968, pb., $1.00 A description of nonviolent demonstrations in Moscow, Sofia, Budapest and Warsaw organized by the War Resisters International against the 1968 Soviet invasion of Czechoslovakia.

11. William Clancy (ed.), **The Moral Dilemma of Nuclear Weapons**. 78pp, 1967, pam., $1.50 A clarification of the moral issues which surround the use of, and the threat to use, nuclear weapons. Includes selections from diverse points of view. The best introduction to the subject.

12. G.H.C. MacGregor, **The New Testament Basis of Pacifism**. 160pp, 1966, pb., $1.25 A theologian carefully analyzes the New Testament to discover its position on the use of mass violence.

13. Gene Sharp, **Exploring Nonviolent Alternatives**. 176pp, 1970, $2.25 Introduction by David Riesman. A realistic appraisal of the techniques of nonviolent action applied to problems of international conflict. Includes an extensive bibliography, eighty-five examples and fifty-one areas for research.

14. Charles Bloomstein (ed.), **From Aid to Development**. 68pp, 1970, pam., $1.50 A special issue of **Intercom** devoted to the problems and prospects of achieving sustained economic growth in modernizing societies in a context of political freedom.

15. G. Ramachandran and T.K. Mahadevan (eds.), **Gandhi, His Relevance for Our Times**. 393pp, 1970, pb., $2.95 An anthology of Western and Indian students of government applying Gandhian ideas of constructive nonviolent conflict to current problems of international relations, nonviolent theory, civil rights activity and nonviolent resistance to aggression. Selections by Joan Bondurant, Gene Sharp, Kenneth Boulding, Charles Walker, Mulford Sibley, R.R. Diwaker and others. Essential reading.

Order From:

> **World Without War Council**
> 1730 Grove Street
> Berkeley, California 94709